The Best Canadian POETRY **2016**

In English

The Best Canadian
POETRY **2016**
In English

Guest Editor
Helen Humphreys

Series Editors
Molly Peacock
Anita Lahey

TIGHTROPE BOOKS

Tightrope Books
#207-2 College Street,
Toronto Ontario, Canada M5G 1K3
tightropebooks.com
bookinfo@tightropebooks.com

SERIES EDITOR: Molly Peacock

GUEST EDITOR: Helen Humphreys

ASSISTANT SERIES EDITOR: Anita Lahey

MANAGING EDITOR: Heather Wood

COPY EDITORS: Jessica Blakemore, Natalie Fuerth, Anderson Tuguinay

COVER DESIGN: Deanna Janovski

COVER ART: Kelley Aitken

INTERIOR DESIGN: David Jang

 Canada Council Conseil des arts
for the Arts du Canada

 ONTARIO ARTS COUNCIL
CONSEIL DES ARTS DE L'ONTARIO
an Ontario government agency
un organisme du gouvernement de l'Ontario

Produced with the assistance of the Canada Council for the Arts and the Ontario Arts Council.

A cataloguing record for this publication is available from Library and Archives Canada. Printed in Canada.

CONTENTS

MOLLY PEACOCK ❧

Foreword

Nine gates of hell, nine choirs of angels, nine months to birth, nine joints on the Taoist bamboo, nine storeys to an Aztec temple, and best of all, nine muses. Nine is the last of the written Arabic numerals, the tying of a knot. Its completeness and its containment of extreme opposites can't help but lead us to poetry, and to our ninth volume of *The Best Canadian Poetry in English*. For years our guest editors have attempted to address the questions raised by our title—the anxiety over what is Best, the defining of what is Canadian—but now the gestation of these ideas leads to the consummate word of our title, poetry itself. Poets are always asked to define—and defend—poetry. Why the need to identify and classify the practice that is called the art of naming, an art that a child so easily recognizes?

In the western world, poets blame Plato. The Greek philosopher was unnerved by the cadenced imagery that "feeds and waters the passions," thoroughly suspicious of the wildness at heart that our guest editor this year, acclaimed poet and novelist Helen Humphreys, describes in her pithy introduction to our volume. Ever since Plato's anxiety, poetry lovers have leapt to explain poetry's magical, rhythmical—and savage—qualities. From Longinus, who gave poets a tremendous boost with "On the Sublime" (commending writers who evoke emotion in their audiences and lauding the intensity of feeling that frightened Plato), all the way down through the centuries to Anita Lahey, our assistant series editor, who contends that poetry does not offer simple, immediate comfort, but is more "like a fire in the hearth that you must leave your bed in the freezing cold to light yourself," lovers of poetry and poets themselves have attempted to define the poetic imagination as they exemplify it.

But even a poet-essayist like Lahey or a poet-fiction writer like Humphreys, both at home in the world of the sentence, still find it a difficult task to translate the world of the line. Emily Dickinson wrote that poetry "Distills amazing sense / From ordinary Meanings" but once that sense is bottled in the poem, it's nearly impossible to turn it back into its ingredients.

One explanation for why the alchemy of rhythms and images can't be reversed comes from the answer to another devilish question poets also agonize over. What is the difference between poetry and prose?

The difference is that a story or a philosophical idea exists *before* words. We can tell the same story (say, that family story everyone repeats at holiday gatherings) in myriad ways. That's because the story exists independently of the telling. Likewise for critical arguments: ideas are *put into* words. Those words form a position to be argued, even as Plato put his fear of rampant emotions into the idea that poetry is suspect.

But unlike stories unfolding in time or ideas maintaining positions, poems do not exist before their words. They exist *only* in their words. The enchantment of the patterned language of a poem lies in the patterned language itself. Curiously, because it exists solely in its words, an ephemeral poem feels eternal.

In rhythms of syllables that have never been composed in exactly this way before, fifty poems have been selected by our guest editor Helen Humphreys, collaborating with Anita Lahey and myself, to represent the best of poetry in English-speaking Canada published online and in print this year. Half of the poets are brand new to our series, and the other half return after a previous appearance or two. No poet has been represented in all nine anthologies, though Karen Solie's work has appeared in the last eight. A.F. Moritz, a former guest editor, happily returns here, and Sylvia Symons steps forth with her first-ever published poem. Our anthology also includes one of the last poems from beloved lyrical poet Elise Partridge, who passed away in 2015.

One of the joys of this book is the personal statement each poet writes. As quirky and original as the poems themselves, the statements are recipes for creativity, providing intimate glimpses into private lives. Tucked away at the back of our book you'll find Alexander Rock's explanation of how he came to the glorious "marriage made in the gutter" when he found Quebec poet Hugo Beauchemin-Lachapelle's poem to translate. Sheri Benning luxuriously describes the comfort of her friend, Stephen Maude comments on how rarely friendship is acknowledged as a source for poetry, while Souvankham Thammavongsa connects childhood friendship with a photograph of a ceiling—and a source for future art. Both Kayla Czaga and Jeff Latosik open fractured windows on childhood experiences of the Internet, while John Terpstra and Tim Bowling consider boyhood. Michelle Good allows us a glimpse of her only son who died, revivified in her poem and in her moving description of how she wrote it. Lawyer Kate Sutherland thinks about the poem as a legal decision, while Armand Garnet Ruffo mulls over indigenous language, nature, and ekphrasis. A number of these poems were conceived as the poet travelled—dislocation prompting poetry for Matt Rader in Cork, Jane Eaton Hamilton in Paris, Gerald Hill in Lisbon, and Laurie D. Graham on Canada's Number One train, even as Tara Michelle Ziniuk writes on ideas of returning home. In a sudden confluence both Maureen Hynes and Steve McOrmond acknowledge debts to American poet James Schuyler. Others among our fifty muse on memory (Douglas Burnet Smith) and idleness (Sally Ito). M. Travis Lane prickles at her source: unwanted advice. Whether it's Cassidy McFadzean connecting Canadian camping with Greek mythology or Stephen Heighton on the life of the double-genre writer, many of the poets yoke seeming opposites. All together their work represents the scope of Canadian poetry as of, well, let's say both the last nine minutes and that peculiar sense of eternity that a good poem conveys. Even Socrates, Plato tells us, began writing poetry in his last days...

Nine apertures in the human body, nine lives to a cat. Some of our poems come to you naked. Others come dressed to the nines. All arrive as the result of the hard work of the editors of the sixty-some print and online journals we scour for this book. These journals are published in every corner of Canada, and we edit this year's anthology from three cities, Kingston, Toronto and Victoria. To lovers of poetry, to newcomers to this art, to the merely curious and the deeply initiated, welcome to Canadian poetry 2016.

Molly Peacock
Toronto, ON

NOTE: Plato, Dialogues, trans. Benjamin Jowett (Oxford, Clarendon, 1871), conveniently also quoted in Parini, Jay, *Why Poetry Matters* (New Haven, Yale University Press, 2008). Some of the symbolic expressions of nine derive from Chevalier, Jean, and Gheerbrant, Alain, *The Penguin Dictionary of Symbols*, trans. John Buchanan-Brown (London, New York, Toronto, Penguin Books, 1996).

ANITA LAHEY ❧

Brace Yourself: The Side Effects of Reading Poetry

I approach poems that are new to me with trepidation, the way children are taught to be wary of strangers. Before steering my eyes to the lines on the page, before taking in the shape of the text and how it's held within the white space, I straighten my posture. Blink, and breathe. I'm dimly aware that I'm preparing my whole self, within and without: girding it. This is not an undertaking for someone fatigued, distracted, or in any way less than alert.

I wouldn't presume that every reader of poetry habitually warms up with a mind-and-body tune-up. But I do believe that the experience of reading a poem, no matter its style or form, no matter the nature of the reader, is fundamentally unlike that of reading prose. The two pursuits are so distinct that to lump both activities under the label of "reading" feels insufficient, even misleading, as if we were to place leaping off the dock into a cottage-country lake on a hot summer afternoon in the same category as diving down deep in a wetsuit, breathing from an oxygen tank, to investigate the lake's ecology.

Think of prose as a string of sentences moving forward. To read those sentences, even those that buck against traditional narrative or linear constructs, is to allow yourself to be led: down the page, over the hills, through the wood. You can follow a line of prose and, on some level, though you are engaged, and may even be changed by what you are reading, you can leave yourself behind. You disappear into the words and the reality they construct, phrase by phrase, moment by moment, along those endlessly wrapping lines of text.

Poetry doesn't offer this sort of escape. Poems, lying there on the page, become physical presences as we read, equipped with real muscle and the ability to use it. We all know what Emily Dickinson said about the top of her head coming off. (It was about more than her head, actually. The full quote, as cited on the Emily Dickinson Museum website, is: "If I read a book and it makes my whole body so cold no fire can warm me I know *that* is poetry. If I feel physically as if the top of my head were taken off, I know *that* is poetry. These are the only way I know it. Is there any other way?") Poems can sit you down, stand you up, spin you in place, turn the space around you upside down or inside out. Sometimes I feel a poem reaching out and pushing back my eyelids, pressing them into the sockets. *Look*, the poem says, into my helplessly bulging eyes. *Look harder, better. There is so much more to see.* I never know what a poem will conjure or contain—or what it will expect from me, its wide-eyed reader.

*

I have been thinking lately about why I turn to poems when I do, and why, sometimes, I don't. When I am desperately worn down, I often read prose, not poetry. Is this OK to admit in a poetry anthology, one I have helped to edit? There's a broadly held sense that poetry provides comfort. There's truth in this. But the kind of solace on offer in poems isn't—for me—typically so effortless to procure as a blanket (or arm) thrown over the shoulders. It's more like that fire in the hearth that you must leave your bed in the freezing cold to light yourself, and that might first require some chopping of kindling, disposing of cinders, even the tricky and hazardous chore of sweeping a filthy chimney. Well worth the effort—magnificent, that fire!—but, well, first there's the effort. To make my way to the place where solace and other treasures await in poems, I need reserves of energy, mental and emotional. I need to feel willing to tumble into that wilderness caught in the poem that guest editor Helen Humphreys describes with such clarity in her introduction to this anthology—to have enough courage (or foolhardiness) on hand for falling headlong into the hole that sometimes lies waiting at a poem's centre, which Seamus Heaney describes in his essay "The Main of Light" as an "unpredictable strike into the realm of pure being."

A strike into the realm of pure being, you say? Wow. Huh! Wonderful, yes, bring it on. Er, um, wait, hold up a sec. I *think* I'm up for that. Maybe later? You know, after supper and a glass of wine. How about after that evening walk we discussed? After my kid's in bed? Sure, OK then! Great, we're set. I'm totally looking forward to it.

In Vancouver author Caroline Adderson's short story "Falling," which appears in her riveting (and funny) collection *Pleased to Meet You*, an underwriter takes the bus to work one morning and accidentally reads a poem, thinking at first that it's one of the advertisements. He's so surprised to find it there, so unprepared for the discovery that people *still write poetry*, that he reads it over and over, puzzling. He gets off at his stop and walks to his office, growing ever more alarmed along the way by the fact that the bus has driven off with the poem. He retrieves two lines from his memory—about falling—and recites them all the way up the elevator to the twenty-seventh floor. He dictates them to the office temp, after which they both let their bodies lean into the floor-to-ceiling windows. They look down. His hands against the glass sweat. He later revisits this moment in a dream, except in the dream world he doesn't notice in time that the windows have been removed. Falling, his dream self enjoys the wind on his face: he feels safe in the knowledge that the poem will catch him.

I reluctantly paraphrase this story—it's so much better told by Adderson—because it captures what can happen when a person enters a poem. Indeed, it's a parable illustrating poetry's possible effects, and as such, it *shows* a great deal of what I am struggling in this essay to *tell*.

The poem first shocks the underwriter awake: it does the job of the coffee he wishes he were drinking. Then it scares him, both its presence and its apparent impenetrability. Yet it holds him under a kind of spell. It's a short one, as all bus poems are: he reads it fifteen times. Though he cannot remember most of the words, the poem has worked its way inside him. It affects his interactions with a coworker, his wife, and his son. It causes him to reach out—into the world, to a stranger—in a way he would never have expected. Having read the poem eventually brings him comfort, alongside a kind of terror, tinged with something he can't explain. He needs the poem, he looks for it, and in the end winds up filling the gaps in his memory—and responding to a potent moment in his own life—with a line he has unknowingly composed himself.

When I encounter a poem for the first time, especially one that grips me, I'm keenly aware I'm taking it in whole on the first, second, fourth and sometimes even tenth read (or bite), distinguishing only the basic ingredients as I chew, and only the most dominant flavours. The poem acts on me in ways that I half-perceive, can barely articulate. And yet it fills me: it causes sensations akin to the cool red berry collapsing between teeth, the warm burn of whiskey down the throat. "Ink runs from the corners of my mouth," the American poet Mark Strand wrote, in one of his all-time best compositions. "There is no happiness like mine. / I have been eating poetry." The more I have read and studied poetry, the more I understand how layered and nuanced the best poems are, how they become impossibly rich meals, serving up fresh courses till you wonder if the dishes and trays will ever stop gliding in and clattering down. I'll be digesting this meal for days, weeks, in some cases years.

This is not meant to frighten the casual reader. Nonetheless, beware: reading poetry is no passive act. To consume a poem is a commitment with unforeseen consequences. It's all-in. Metaphors ring and reverberate. Phrases morph into earworms. Imagery implants. Attached to them all: a sense of power and meaning you intuit but cannot fully parse. You are held. And there's work to be done. You can close the final page on a collection of poems, but you'll never be able to say to yourself, "There. The story is over."

The end of the poem is not the end of anything at all.

*

The first poem in this year's anthology, by virtue of its author's last name, is James Arthur's "A Local History." It's a free-verse composition of formally shaped three-line stanzas that opens with "My grandmother's house," a simple phrase loaded with clues: Arthur is leading his reader into a world of memories, familial, familiar. Right away, I'm suspicious. I'm thinking: been there, done that. But by the end of the first line, I'm jolted out of my cynicism. This is no archetypal grandmother, but a real one, with a houseful of flies. She doesn't fit the mold. Of course, pretty much no one "fits the mold," but this is a truth that bears revisiting, for reasons I can never satisfactorily define.

This is where I've gone in line one of Arthur's poem: far off from its plain statement into my prejudices and those that swirl around me, then straight down into my longstanding struggle with this underlying, persistent fact of human nature. As I read on, I sense my emerging mood fitting right into the poem, where another distressing scenario is playing out: the flies are crawling over each other on the windowsill, they're "spinning out their noisy dying," and "you could sweep forever / and not get all the dead flies off the floor." We're only in the second stanza but I'm already so inside this poem and its rhythms that I instantly become the body sweeping the flies. I feel the broom in my hands and hear the brush of bristles on the floor as I swing back-and-forth in that fluid, universal sweeping motion, conscious of the fly carcasses sticking with tangles of dust in the broom's ends, which I will later have to pull free with my fingers.

This communion between the poem and the body crops up again and again in discussions of the form. In an essay on falling in love with poetry, a wonderful occasional series in *The New Quarterly*[1], Isabel Huggan (a celebrated prose author as well as an alumnus of this anthology) places her first joyful experience of poetry squarely on the bouncing foot of an uncle reciting a rollicking verse not entirely suitable for a child. Later, when she has progressed to Tennyson's "The Lady of Shallot," she tells us, "I simply experienced the effect the poem created in my body, thoughtless as to its origins. As earlier in childhood, my relationship to language was kinetic."

Kinetic: "of or relating to motion." The language and its rhythms move through and act upon the reader: this is palpable, physical, not just the mind alone churning away up there in the literary clouds; not alone the ineffable response of an elusive soul. "This is the way the ladies ride," Amanda Jernigan writes, and repeats, and repeats again, in her poem "Engraving" in this volume, and I am galloping in place, steering clear, I hope, of the "whinging devil and the menacing old man." A few pages later, in "A Little Advice from the Matriarch," M. Travis Lane proposes "Don't hold your nose while passing God. / A letter has been sent to you." And I'm reaching into the mailbox; sauntering past a deity; sniffing out a holy aroma—all to Lane's tetrameter beat. In his book, *How to Read a Poem and Fall in Love With Poetry*, Edward Hirsch points out how W.B. Yeats once claimed in a poem, "I made it out of a mouthful of air." Hirsch leads from this to a description of the reader's remaking of the poem with his or her *own* breath: "When I recite a poem I reinhabit it, I bring the words off the page into my own mouth, my own body… I let its verbal music move through me as if the poem is a score and I am its instrumentalist . . . I let its heartbeat pulse through me…"

The poem read aloud stirs in the lungs and mouth, in breath, and travels on from there. I'd argue that the poem may be just as potent even if read silently, and I'm not alone. In yet another of those wonderful TNQ essays, the exuberant and exacting Quebec poet Bruce Taylor jumps off from T.S. Eliot's notion of the auditory imagination, that "feeling for syllable and rhythm, penetrating far below the conscious levels of thought and feeling, invigorating every word." In his own prose, Taylor writes, "It is true, the imagination—narrowly seen as the ability to form mental images of things not present—belongs to the ear as well as the eye, calling up voices from the quiet page. But there is also an oral imagination, and when we read a poem, we speak it inwardly, with the mind's mouth."

[1] Several of these essays are now collected in the anthology *Falling in Love with Poetry*, edited by former TNQ editor Kim Jernigan and released in spring 2016. The anthology is available at tnq.ca.

How we "speak" in our minds when we read poetry is different from any other way we read or use language. In her pensive and illuminating book of prose, *Personal History*, Toronto poet Roo Borson writes, "Poetry is made of words, yet it is exactly as articulate as music, and as distinct from ordinary speech. Spoken in a near monotone, the motion of thought is its real melody." I'm not sure I agree that poetry's score need be so narrow (though many poets *do* read their work aloud in just that register, "near monotone"), but the "motion of thought" is worth dwelling on, as well as the idea that poetry is as "articulate" as music. Poetry functions within its own ecosystem of sense and sound, a system of overlapping techniques and flourishes that's impossible to parse without losing the effects you are trying to solve. For a poet to follow the "motion of thought"—so layered, so unruly, and so persistently on-the-go, often switching directions before we've fully grasped where it's been—is profoundly difficult work. To hold, portray and reenact that journey within a text is tougher still, especially to do so in a way that includes all the necessary signposts for a reader to tag along.

Let's go back to where we were, sweeping dead flies in James Arthur's poem. Reading on, following the poem's "motion of thought," I come, I hardly know how, to an idea that may be the clue to the metaphor in the persistent flies. You could sweep forever, I think, and not get rid of the bodies, the brutal histories, the lost lives. Do the old ones eventually disappear? It's impossible to know for sure, because there are always more, endlessly more.

By now I've spent real time in the complex reality of Arthur's poem, following its trail of images: cracking milkweed pods, Saxon kings, a father's father's ashes, Roman aqueducts, a wall of suburban snow, a famously missing horse and rider who, just by being mentioned, appear vividly in the mind's eye. These disparate images would seem random or incongruous outside the poem, but here they feel inevitable, even obvious. They fit. Why? I propose that it's partly the succession of hard, clipped sounds that phrases like "bristle-sided reeds" and "wrenched up" and "weed-choked" and "grave-goods" make in the "mind's mouth" that Bruce Taylor writes of. It's partly that we trust the poet, though the route he lays out for us is meandering and strange, because his voice and use of language are sure and clear. It's partly the build-up in my visual imagination of a harsh and littered landscape, a build-up that is occasionally interrupted with softer, more intimate asides: "Something I read in college / and for whatever reason have not forgotten." Despite feeling more gentle and open-ended, even vague, a line like this speaks of a helplessness in the face of knowledge and memory: what sticks is not under our control. It's a shift in rhythm, a breather, the poet reaching through his own litany to appeal to us directly in a way that underlines the unrelenting violence in the sounds and imagery piling up all around.

The poem turns out to be not simply an ode to a grandmother—though it definitely gives due to a "hard old woman" who habitually skinny-dipped in a freezing pond—but a "local history" that plunges us into a frothing pool of histories from far-off lands and times, hardships here and wars there, all of it a-bubble in the ground beneath our feet. For me, the poem is a reminder that we are intimately connected to the whole trajectory of human history. This is how history repeats itself; this is the original globalism; this is all of us, from our grandmothers' kitchens outward, implicated in what's gone before and what's to come. By the end of reading (and rereading) this poem, I understand I'm kin with "late arrivers" through time, with "*after-folk* living on the graves of a greater folk.*"

I should clarify: this understanding lodged in me on my first reading of Arthur's poem. I felt it. But I can only attempt to articulate it after many readings. That's what happens with well-crafted poems: the effects of reading them are rich, layered, subliminal. They do cast spells. In the case of "A Local History," with the hypnotic music of lines like "*after-folk* living on the graves of a greater folk" and so many others enfolding me, arming me, thrumming in time with my own internal rhythms, I'm prepared by the end of the poem— as has been the fate of all peoples "annihilated, / assimilated, or driven into the sea", as was likewise the fate of the grandmother—to lose my words, my house, my name. I know such losses are inevitable, whether by the actions of my fellow humans or by death. And I can't say why, but for just this moment, my eyes resting on the shore of the sea at the bottom of this poem, I'm ready.

Ready for death, defeat, destruction. Boy does that sound depressing. And yet I'm not discouraged, not a bit. I'm awed, I'm perplexed, I'm frightened and—yes—amid it all, I'm comforted. Discombobulated, but somehow whole, and wow. This sense of wholeness will pass, but to find it at all: bliss! relief! In *Personal Histories*, Borson quotes a passage from American poet Robert Creeley and asks, "What is it I'm hearing here? The non-existent rain? Or is it that Creeley's poem brings me back to myself, that on reading it I know once more, without trying, what and where I am, literally: here, now, this body, this air."

Borson is grounded by the poem: she finds her way home. So the act of reading poetry translates as motion toward stillness. Movement back to the self, in time and space. And always, ever, these contradictions when we talk poetry. Molly Peacock, this anthology's heroic series editor—also its visionary founding editor—writes in her deliciously insightful book *How to Read a Poem... and Start a Poetry Circle* of the "curious combination of being both delighted and stymied" that she came to identify early on with reading poetry. "To be comfortable with many inexplicable meanings," she writes, "yet to be able to find meaning, to actively locate it in a syllable, a beat, an image, and to have clarity and mystery at the same time—that seems to define the complete way to live." What power and excitement there is, in gripping hold of meaning in the midst of all the confusion that defines daily life. This may be precisely where poetry's comfort germinates: the poem offers a framework within which to carry on this daunting and seemingly futile work of seeking meaning, a defined mental and emotional space where, if even for a half-second, an in-breath or an out, we can say to ourselves, or feel in our bones, ever so tentatively: *ah, yes, this.*

At the very moment of contact, of course, "this" falls right through us and disintegrates. "Each time any of us reads a favourite poem," Peacock writes, "it conjures a special sorcery of second sight, and third, and fourth, until understanding is so profound that we are returned to a state before we even had language—a prelinguistic place. That's why it is so hard to say exactly what a poem means. Like being stupidly in love, this art leaves you dumbstruck."

So. The poem puts words in your mouth, your mind, your entire being—*words* that actually strike you dumb. It "moves you" while bringing you back to yourself, putting you in your place, as it were. If I have learned one indisputable thing over the years, it's that poetry and paradox are sisters. A poem is never one thing, but several things at once, some of which by rights should cancel each other out as you read along. Somehow, they never do.

*

James Arthur's "A Local History" was not the first poem among the 50 selected here that I encountered. (All poems are read in the publications where they first appeared, whenever those publications happen to circulate among the anthology's guest and series editors.) Nonetheless, Arthur's poem hits notes that sound again and again throughout this year's selection like little refrains: it seems, now, from its place at the front of the alphabet, to set a tone. This is a noteworthy side effect of bringing together such a powerful grouping. The poems' proximity to one another, their accidental order, causes interactions between them as their voices mingle in a reader's mind.

For me, the braiding of memory, history and geography—so thickly and tautly twisted in this first poem—reoccurs with increasing resonance, while at the same time tying a kind of double-braid with my personal macramé of time, tale and place. I'm thinking of the fathers' tractors in the field reminiscent of "their fathers' Paschendaele" in Tim Bowling's "Tetherball," a poem that breaks out into a litany of metaphors for useless violence, including the protest of another not-to-be-trifled-with grandmother (this one chained to a Douglas fir). My own grandmother escaped her country just in time (different war), filled and refilled a deep freezer with loaves of zucchini bread, and scrubbed walls into her 90s, when she was just this side of lame. She lived by an almost violent willfulness and rejection of sentiment that was occasionally tempered by tenderness. She rears, at times full-force, as I wade through these roiling poetic landscapes. She once told me learning Polish was a waste of time— "Difficult language, you soon forget!"—but when she couldn't dissuade me from visiting the old country, she sent me off with two sets of money-stuffed envelopes: one for distribution among her living relatives, the other to spend on flowers for the graves of her dead ones. Bowling's tetherball says "'It's hard. Life's hard,' / and we get up from our stalled tractor / to punch above our weight /and the tetherball takes it and / gives it back—". My grandmother scrubbing, resisting; me grasping at a language her family's dislocation caused to die. Memory, history, geography.

The American author Francine Prose writes in her book *Reading Like a Writer* about a "confrontation with the mystery of time." She's referring to the experience of encountering notes in her own handwriting from long ago, evidence of a familiar but distant self. But any tour through poetic literature past and present is littered with such confrontations. The way time and place collapse within poems, and by extension within readers of poems, is a marvellous feat, the effect of which is akin to what happens when you stand atop a table in a familiar room, but magnified. Light shifts, shadows move, objects claim more or less space. Nothing has changed but your own position, and that is everything. The narrator in John Steffler's "I Haven't Looked at These in Years" declares—the discovery is startling and redemptive— "my beloved father was human, here's his hand holding / his knife, it's how I still remember him." In these lines we see, through our combined powers of imagination, the father, the hand, and even the speaker of the poem holding the photograph, staring. Where has he kept it all these years? Why has it reemerged now? Who took the photo? Who else was in the room?

The room—what of the room? The reclamation of the house in Julie Bruck's "Flipped" from the demolition it succumbed to outside the page is so vivid, a little subdivision of my own past homes pops up around it as I read, creating a neighbourhood of memory and loss. I'm gripped by the magic through which Bruck's words give the very gift they proclaim necessary, simply by naming it, and situating it precisely: "To imagine / the next part of the journey requires at least one / small daschund, black as an olive, asleep / at the centre of the sunny rug since 1957." And boy, have I crossed that "cantilever of intimacy / and threat" in Dorothy Fields' "Geography of Memory," in which an attempt to connect becomes the "treacherous sway from / one side of the canyon to the other," in which the geography of a relationship is so deftly—again, inexplicably redemptively—situated in a seemingly unrelated yet wholly appropriate landscape.

And so. I nod encountering Randy Lundy's memory as "the old ache in the knee." I latch onto the wistful, sorrowful dream of transformation in Michelle Good's "Defying Gravity": "If I were a river / I would be blue and brown and green at once; / clear as glass, the stones bright, light, a rusty refraction. / Would you swim in me again?" On the banks of another river, the narrator in Steven Heighton's poem "In Order to Burn" resists the memory-road back to a love affair: "the couple you made is still current / on that earth," Heighton writes, and because the setting is "a certain cold river" where "the birches are in full business / and the grass of the banks is wild mint" the word "current" hums with suggestion and innuendo. Resistance is futile, as the poem's existence proves. Instead, it offers a prescription for memory embedded in place embedded in self: "You were conscious, then, / even sleeping, and what's wholly lived keeps looping."

I hope that's true—that Heighton knows of what he speaks—when I revisit the anticipation of grief in Joelle Barron's "This Job Ends in Six Months." This poem's stricken narrator carries a child "through subdivision bones, suburbia / purpling around us," she drives around the "block's strange layers / of city on ocean on farm." I'm kicked, by sheer force of the sadness rising from the poem's "hot breath," back to my own childhood suburban street: I haunt it in my mind, feeling for the "distant watery light of us" that the narrator hopes will tuck away quietly in the child. Do I have such a gentle, fuzzy memory? Who would inhabit it?

Maybe not the person I'd wish had been there. And if not, when you get right down to it, would that matter? In "Wish You Were Here," Jane Eaton Hamilton's wry, cuttingly humorous collection of "postcards," the narrator reminds us,

> ... we will all be dead
> in a few decades at most, and then
> whether or not I wanted you here
> will really be moot, as will, of course
> the discussion of whether I am a
> charming psychopath, a witch or a narcissist
> or even just an ordinary woman with a brain
> that causes me to think.

Dangerous stuff, thinking. Go down that road, you might just tear open that infamous hole with its direct view into "the realm of pure being." Which looks how, exactly? Hamilton accuses the recipient of her satiric travelogue, "You were always pointing at something outside the frame."

That, that, is where my eye is drawn when reading the work of our poets: outside the frame. And the other eye? Suddenly able to go its own way, it focuses dead centre. The rest of me, the *all of me* taking in these contrasting and somehow overlapping views, stands in place, swaying, readjusting, relishing an unexpected breeze, the source of which is unclear. "'Tyger, Tyger Burning Bright' and 'Kubla Khan' crashed through to me when I was about 10 or 12," P.K. Page once wrote (in her own "Falling in Love with Poetry" essay). "I had no idea what either of them meant. I had no need to know. I still don't know."

Anita Lahey
Victoria, BC

HELEN HUMPHREYS ❧

Wild at Heart

It is not form, or lack of form, or intellectual fervor, or exquisite lyricism that makes a good poem in my world, but rather it is a poem that has a little piece of wilderness at its heart. What I mean by "wilderness" is that there is a quality or aspect to the poem that exists because of the poem itself, not because it was orchestrated or carefully inserted there by the poet. This "wilderness" is something that has taken the poet by surprise and therefore also takes the reader by surprise, and it is this small turn, this surprise, that makes both poet and reader forget themselves and fully enter the world of the poem. And it is this forgetting, this immersion, that makes a poem really sing, that makes it successful. A poem that has our full attention has earned it by doing something unexpected, by opening towards wilderness, rather than towards safety and convention. And to achieve this, a poet has to be unafraid to take risks, unafraid to open towards the unknown, unafraid to examine their material with brutal honesty. This is always hard to do because it requires effort and, and it is hard to maintain because the effort cannot ever be lessened.

Good writing is a delicate balance of receptivity and control. Receptivity is a willingness to explore and experiment, to be vulnerable to life and all its teachings. This is often the province of the young, and it is no accident that, historically, many of the best poems have been written when the poets were at the beginning of their lives. This is generally a time of natural openness, and it is also when the first strong emotions are experienced. First times, first feelings have been the favourite subjects of young poets since the beginning of time itself.

But how does one remain receptive after youth has passed? It is a question of seeking rather than resting, of constantly pushing oneself further, into places that are unfamiliar and where there is risk involved. The best writing exposes the vulnerabilities of the writer, doesn't keep them hidden, and in the way that much of life is paradoxical, the vulnerability becomes the strength of the work. Think of the poems in Sylvia Plath's, *Ariel*, for example.

Control is craft and the mastery of technique. It comes from years of practice, from failing and making better, from trying and trying again. Control comes with age and practice. The trick is not to gain control at the expense of remaining open, because control without openness to balance it will result in poetry that is stiff and predictable.

The poems in this anthology are ones where I feel the poet has achieved this difficult balance between control and receptivity, and where the poem has a kernel of wilderness at its heart. These were all poems that took my full attention, that surprised me, and where the reading of the poem was an entirely immersive experience. I lived for a moment in their brief, wild hearts, and I savoured them. My hope is that when you read them here, in these pages of *Best Canadian Poetry in English 2016*, you will enjoy them as much as I did.

Helen Humphreys
Kingston, ON

Details and Rules for the Best Canadian Series

This year, the fifty best poems and the list of notable poems were selected from more than sixty print and online journals, a list of which appears in the final pages of this book. No poems may be submitted directly to the anthology. All poems chosen must be published in the previous year in a Canadian print or online periodical. We depend on those periodicals to keep us updated on their issues.

Acknowledgements

This series owes a special debt to Tightrope publisher, Jim Nason, and to our managing editor, Heather Wood. We could not have produced the series without her thoroughness and good humour. Our gratitude goes to David Jang for interior design, Jessica Blakemore, Natalie Fuerth, and Anderson Tuguinay for copyediting and proofreading, and to Deanna Janovski for our cover look. We are particularly grateful to this year's cover artist, Tightrope author, Kelley Aitken. Each year we hold a "Best Friends" celebration to support our enterprise, and we thank Kali Hewitt-Blackie, Jeff Kirby and Lois Lorimer for their dedication to this event.

The Editors

The Best Canadian
POETRY **2016**
In English

JAMES ARTHUR ❧

A Local History

My grandmother's house was always full of flies.
They'd crawl across each other on the windowsill
or would be spinning out their noisy dying

everywhere—so many, you could sweep forever
and not get all the dead flies off the floor.
Downhill, in a marsh of bristle-sided reeds,

milkweed pods kept cracking open, leaking seed
across the air, renewing the existence of their species
in the way they'd done from year to year.

Way back when, some hard-handed
Methodist pioneer had somehow wrenched up
every stone big enough to break a plough

and piled them all throughout the woods,
where they still were, in mounds, when I was growing up,
like barrows heaped above the decomposed

remains of the violent Saxon kings, whose grave-goods
featured large in my imagination.
My grandmother's gone. Before she died

she lost her words, her house, her name.
But for me, she's still a hard old woman
walking downhill at dawn, long into autumn,

to skinny-dip in her weed-choked, freezing pond.
A hedge of wind, a wall of suburban snow—
my father's father's ashes are in the ground

in southern Ontario. Something I read in college
and for whatever reason have not forgotten
is that the ancient Saxon barrow-makers, living

among broken things they could admire
but not rebuild—aqueducts and roads the Romans
left behind—saw themselves as late arrivers, as

an *after-folk* living on the graves of a greater folk
who'd gone before. Where is the horse, where
the rider, some now-nameless Saxon

wrote, grieving for a people who his own
people centuries before had annihilated,
assimilated, or driven into the sea.

from *Hazlitt*

JOELLE BARRON ❧

This Job Ends in Six Months

for Jack

You won't remember how we sometimes
sat on the kitchen floor eating berries
from a steel mixing bowl. People won't
smile the way they did on our walks;
matching skin in that city made us mother and son.
Maybe the smell of playground bark,
or the sudden cold of dusk on metal
will make you feel a faraway thing,
but you won't know how I carried you
home through subdivision bones, suburbia
purpling around us. Your breath hot
against my neck, how alone we were. How
I put you in the car, drove circles around
the dyke, your block's strange layers
of city on river on farm. *Mamama*
tumbling from your wet lips, making
me remember that once, I was almost
a mother. I hope in the deep of whoever
you become, there will be the distant,
watery light of us. Tension that left
your body as I held you
against me, as you fell asleep.

from *Arc Poetry Magazine*

HUGO BEAUCHEMIN-LACHAPELLE ❧

translated by Alexander Rock

Untitled

from Poème Sale, *2014*

A custodian is polishing
ingots with a
rag redeemed from the trash

budget cuts
have forced him to wash
the economy's
filthy windows
with filthy water

so that
nobody
will see
without

from *The Puritan*

Northern Rockies

Spruce beetles creaking through a stand of five sickly spindlies. Eerie as a campfire tale, the one where the killer's going scritch, scritch, scritch. The precursor of slow tires on gravel.

Next door, a French couple cycling down from Anchorage. Next door, an elderly terrier, standing and shaking out before flopping herself down. Next door, a motorcyclist with a sack of trail mix. Next door, a military family moving up to Anchorage with teacup poodles named Buddy and Cool Whip.

How do you know you've been here long enough? When you recognize the types of travellers, when they recognize you at the grocery store, when you dream of your own hometown, its sounds and smells and the time you quit your job at sixteen and the boss said he'd see to it you never worked in this town again. Well, you're working in this town again? You and the spruce · beetles, creaking away.

from *Lemon Hound*

Vigil
to Yi-Mei Tsiang

I am no longer young. I know
what we love, we will lose.
Your head resting in my lap
as you hold your newborn
to your open breasts, milk scent,
mown hay. Snow falls
beneath the street lamp's glow,
flutter of her eyelashes as you nurse
her into dreams of light and shadow.
I read in the tow of candles we lit
to mark this evening's coming.
With my free hand I gloss dark waves
of your hair. All I want is to unknot
what anchors you here, to ease you
into sleep. If I could read the notes
of your new mother's heartbeat
that I feel against my thighs,
they'd be a lullaby—
   Don't be afraid.
  We love what we will lose.
I am not young anymore.
Your body sighs, you slip
into sleep's undertow,
the anchor rope,
tossed to shore.

from *EVENT*

Tetherball

It isn't played much anymore. My kids don't play.
I don't play for nostalgia.
But well I remember that lump in the throat
of the agues of autumn
no day could swallow—on the schoolyard cement
in slanting rain, a scarecrow of iron
with its head lopped off, dangling, waiting
for some kid to smash it in the face
as if it were the abominated classroom clock
above the desks stalled in the hours
like our fathers' tractors in the muddied
potato fields so like their fathers' Paschendaele
they weren't alike at all.

You wrapped the leather ball
around the pole by punching it
against another's punches
or your own, a purely democratic
violence of the kind
the world teaches every one
of us, in time. Useless—
the monk setting fire to his flesh
to free his people
the grandmother chained to a Douglas Fir
to save a saw-whet owl's song
the writer of twenties noir
soldered to the keys of his Underwood
inspired by Joyce—useless.

Yet there's the tetherball in the compound.

A bully
who has no victim
but himself, a tree
stripped by acid rain,
a one-armed boxer with a single glove.

Did I say I didn't play? Who doesn't play?
In all weather, out there,
the tetherball says "It's hard. Life's hard,"
and we get up from our stalled tractor
to punch above our weight
and the tetherball takes it and
gives it back—old confessor,
grounded bolt, imploded gourd

maypole of our solitudes and prison yard.

from *The Fiddlehead*

Flipped

The Laurentian home my parents built in 1957 became
too much for my mother. Alone in her 80s, she treated
its sale like the placement of a beloved pet—she wouldn't

trust just *anyone*. Realtors grew testy as she spurned offers
from people with plans, buyers with improvements in mind.
Years until she approved the couple from Ottawa, who lived

there for a month, told neighbors they didn't like the view.
The house sat empty, drooped with Christmas lights through
two Julys. My mother lost touch. They tore the house down.

On Google Earth, its replacement could shelter a cult
with two swimming pools and a taste for *contemporary
elegance/open concept/ lounge bar/wine cellar/grotto.*

With a four-car garage and paving that begins at the new
security gates, pressing back the pines and birches
like unruly demonstrators, only the clouds look familiar.

The property's listed as a *Single Family Home.*
We thought our mother crazy, trying to control the house's
future when her own life was slipping from her grasp.

Now, I tear through albums and boxes of old photos,
finding none of the place we called *The Red Door*—not
snow-capped in winter, nor thronged with the wildflowers

she reseeded by the fistful each spring—that riot,
their chaos—which she loved. No sign of how we lived.
Mornings in her city apartment, my mother struggles

at her walker, someone beside her, another behind.
Her heels don't touch the floor, and it takes a desperate
dancing to stay up on the balls of her thin, confused feet.

Suppose that couple had loved her house as she did,
had known how light crossed its rooms differently
in each season, or conversed with those red-eyed

night visitors who peered through the screen doors—
could my mother's wiring have also endured?
A child's wish. But the house was her memory:

She needed it well-tended, even after she'd walked
away. A mind wants a place to return to. To imagine
the next part of the journey requires at least one

small dachshund, black as an olive, asleep
at the center of the sunny rug since 1957.
A cold drink sweating beside my father's chair.

from *The Rusty Toque*

Dream Jobs

Random Link Clicker.

Royal Bath Taker.
Receiver of Foot Rubs and Praise.

Chief Executive Napper.

Undersecretary of Trivial Pursuits.

Jester to Her Empirical Majesty of Unverifiable Facts.
Procurer of Unnecessary Hats.

Empress of Ice Cream.

Cloud-Development Supervisor.
Inspector General of Minor Slights.
Editorial Dictator-in-Residence.
Bubble Blower to the Stars.

from *The Walrus*

Black Sea Nettle

If the relationship to one's body is expressed
algebraically, let every variable be a decorative
tuber. A golden mean of worry buried
by one animal and dug up by another.

What's tucked up or down and not talking?
Consider the colour, the space of days
between what we know to be good, other,
or another and decide. The story of a woman

who cut her foot and died within five hours.
She was pregnant, or had a tumour. It was
a black spot on her left shin after having
mown the lawn. During an eclipse,

she looked at the sun without her
daughter's pinhole camera. She was
a neighbour who hadn't washed her hands
after breaking eggs for bread pudding.

She was eighty-five, unmarried, no
children. Mail snowed the summer
door until they found her. She was never
born. It was her fault. It won't happen

again. During a date, the other woman
offers that she exists in a medical textbook
in England. Parts of her collapsed
early. A bottle in, she invites you

to feel how the small bones are fused
like mercury. This is a fairytale where
the woodman's axe draws the wrong blood.
Except the woodsman is you. Is also her.

Sheet stain and the indifferent shrug
of something you can do without,
but are you sure? You've made a blood
oath with so many things some days

your body begs to follow. From the inside
out, jellyfish, the soft slip of fingers, tentacle
reversal. A confusing of predatory intent.
Once teenaged, in the back of a red Renault

in Chrysler country, the driver stared
into the flat tooth of his rearview mirror
and said, *I don't trust anything
that bleeds for five days and doesn't die.*

Modestine

We have each tried to read to him, with no success, except for James,
who read him all of Robert Louis Stevenson's *Travels with a Donkey in
the Cévennes*

I was there, in the first of the long-term care centres, when he finished
the story,

And we all shared the narrator's sadness about giving up his donkey,

Not having realized that he loved her; unable to retrieve her
I was lying beside him, listening to the sounds of small, solid hooves and

A tin bell, my father's good breathing

The kinds of sounds that strike like hammers, later on in life

He was better then: my phone reminder CALL DAD still appears each
night at

Eight, but there are no phones where he is now, no nurses to plead with to
let me

Speak to him, and anyway, he will have been asleep for hours

We talked every night for months, then less and now

I wait until my mother, sister, or brother is there, and have short, stilted

Talks that end either in tears or furious impatience

He has stopped talking about his cat, or his own bed

And asks some questions over and over, while swerving in and out of sense

The donkey's feelings are not evoked in the book;

The author also thrashed the abused creature, and God only knows

How she fared with her new owner: inside of her is the baby she was,

Learning to stand, then endure, enduring all

Please let me go home? my father said out of the blue, not too long ago

I'll be quiet; I won't bother anyone

Please, he said, again but so quietly, having been beaten down,

Having seen nothing but the dark, interminable road ahead

Diminish into a short path, governed by

certainties that fly right past him,

By grace itself, by its absence and outrage.

from *The Walrus*

LIVEJOURNAL.COM/LONELYRADIO

We could read your words from anywhere
but you felt like the only soul sitting
in your swivel chair listening to your parents

dream-breathing down the hall, typing to boys
from Kelowna and Trinidad about
your boredom and body. You blogged

about the three-legged moose you saw
on the highway to Terrace, the lonely red radio
light on top of a mountain. A boy

from Michigan called you on the phone.
His voice reminded you of a tv show. It was
dawn there, Detroit already falling

like an ancient empire. In the photo he sent,
his face was obscured by a trucker hat.
Was the Internet a series of tubes or something

scientists kept in a room in California? Did a robot
army of spiders weave its connections?
In every post, you were the lonely red radio light

we could see from the airport but never get
close to. You gave virtual blowjobs, saw how
other kids in other towns cut themselves, how other

kids walked around other ice rinks
with their problems and frenemies. After school
you completed different versions of the same.

What's your favourite colour? Sometimes yellow,
mostly red. Who's your best friend? What's the one
thing you'll never forget? Listen to me,

Lonely Radio, I sat behind you in Spanish.
Your hair kept changing colours—black, purple,
black, red—it was a beautiful lightshow I burnt out

after lunch to. Years later, an online boy you loved
was shot dead by his teenage wife. Another
Internet friend messaged you about it. You read

about it, could see the wife's photo but not
his. Listen, Lonely Radio, you haven't written
in a while. I think of you every time I fly

from Terrace with Styrofoam coffee and the sun
closing red behind the mountains—please
write, please tell us that you're fine.

from *The Puritan*

The Geography of Memory

My mother doesn't forget—reminds me how
a friend and I made spritz cookies from *The Joy of Cooking*
how the electric mixer splattered dough all over the kitchen walls.
Sixty years ago. I've come east for her ninety-fifth birthday.
She's forgotten my friend's name but I haven't, maybe
because she's reminded me so many times. My mother
never made cookies, never splattered batter. Nor did she
have to clean up the mess. Other women did that.

She asks again if I ever hear from the husband I am without,
twelve years now. Each time she sees me. No. The answer
doesn't change. No longer asks if that husband's sister's children
ever see their Black father? The answer was always: No.
Asks if my oldest friend has a "companion" meaning lover, meaning
woman. Yes, I say, these last ten years. How is it she can remember

the spritz cookies but not the more tender things?
And if I lied, changed my answer, would she notice?
My mother probes me, a tongue to a painful gum,
my sins, my loss, the vagrancy of my friends

and me. Is this how she builds bridges? A cantilever of intimacy
and threat like those gap-toothed spans I walked
over Nepal's fierce rivers, the Dudh Kosi, the Kali Gandaki,
a few cables, some boards, half missing, a treacherous sway from
one side of the canyon to the other, a milky spume of river below.
Glue your eyes to the far bank. Don't look down. Don't
breathe. Just keep walking.

from *FreeFall*

Lifecycle of the Mole-Woman: Infancy as a Human

I've seen this waist-high grass
and weeping tree before, in a drugstore frame
and a Bollywood movie, the trunk a pivot point
for coquettish hide and seek. On the cover
of *Vanity Fair* it had a swing,
just two ropes and a plank, a girl levitating
on the tip of her coccyx. Poofy virginal
white dress, elegant lipstick slash, Cubist chin,
she had it all. Someone proposed here,
votive candles in a heart, a flowered trellis;
it went viral on the internet and spawned
a thousand thousand proposals. Someone
has decided this is a place where no one
can be ugly, this lonely hillside that bears
but one tree, one strand of sweet grass,
summer sun fixed at one low angle,
stuck like broken spotlight. The branches
ache to be free of their heavy greenery,
to winter for once. Shorn, fallen, and bare.

from *Carousel*

Defying Gravity

So many rivers we wandered without helmsman or guide.
    Some so shallow the stones barely below the surface,
        glacier shrapnel once jagged, now tumbled round and smooth.
        Others, honey rivers wide and slow, the breeze
rich with warm clover.
    They made us light in their embrace, these rivers,
whether our bodies splayed them open
    or we lay beside them laughing in key with the timeless
rumble of water and stone; If I were a river
        I would be blue and brown and green at once;
           clear as glass, the stones bright, light, a rusty refraction.
        Would you swim in me again?
Would you ride the river inside me as you once did?
Could we both be born over in a rushing river of light and hope?
I wish I were a river.

from *The Puritan*

LAURIE D. GRAHAM ❧

Number One Canadian

Stutter-stepping, the last fumes
out of Ontario, beds and sliding doors and dining cars

tunnelling through the forest,
its genealogy of clear-cut,

its firework trees hot and new.
We show them our ghost station, we show them tea at the window

as birch die over power lines,
birch hauling lines down to the level of marsh

and marsh rising up to meet electricity.
There's no other *this* to this.

This is the track: a propane tank every fifty clicks,
wall-eyed shoots and utility corridors,

gift-buying hours in the recreation car,
hints of water and smoke, if you're looking for them.

No Oh my Nation, no God Save our Queen,
no colonial imperative except in our being here,

in what it means to shower
on a moving train, rolling track

under the drainhole, the luxurious pillows,
my last-minute discount: this

is what we starved a people for, this dying, comfortable journey,
and the tree-planters paying off their student loans, their blisters an economy

of impatience—the travellers will grow impatient
rounding the big lakes, they'll buy the wild blueberries,

they'll take photos of each other beside abandoned buildings along the line,
they'll stiffen up in the dome car and watch the last light leave

and wonder why we're stopped, why we're waiting again,
for every single freight train, waiting, middle of nowhere.

from *Prairie Fire*

Wish You Were Here

1

Or I don't. I can't decide—
do I wish you were here
or am I glad that you aren't here
or do I feel too little of anything
and if I do, does it matter since, really
it's inescapable, we will all be dead
in a few decades at most, and then
whether or not I wanted you here
will really be moot, as will, of course
the discussion of whether I am a
charming psychopath, a witch or a narcissist
or even just an ordinary woman with a brain
that causes me to think

2

It is pleasant here in England/Spain/Greece/China/
Namibia/Tanzania/Cuba/Colombia/Japan/
New Zealand/Thailand/Indonesia
The cows in the fields chew their cuds
(cows are cows are cows)
In the cities, linguistics bounce through air
(languages are languages are languages)

3

I am still as
  a) stubborn
  b) ignorant
  c) mercenary

as I always was, however
and I wish you were here
so that we could go dancing
I would be happy to report that
I have changed, but I haven't changed

4

I think of you a lot, and especially of the time you—
And also that once when you—
And of course about the time we—

5

Look, though, penguins climbed across my stomach
A flock of lorikeets landed on my arms
A croc reared on its hind legs but didn't attack
A kiwi pecked across a beach at 3 a.m.
I went up in a hot air balloon
I wore a kimono

6

Really, I think of you all the time
(except for when I'm not thinking of you)

7

I have a photograph, bent, its corner torn
We stand beside a pool
gone brackish with winter and seagulls
in heavy coats, scarves, red Canada mittens
You point towards something in the sky
just outside the frame

You were always pointing at something
just outside the frame

8

I dreamed I got a postcard from you delivered to poste restante
Having a fabulous time
Glad you aren't here

9

I miss you or perhaps I don't miss you
and when I walk down into the Paris metro
and see fervently heterosexual lovers kissing
I think of you bending to my neck—
or perhaps I don't think of you
and instead only wish I had a decent camera

A John Lennon look-alike shuffles cards
A man plays La Vie en Rose on the accordion
A homeless man sits with a slice of white bread hanging from his mouth
When I get off at my stop, a lemon
rolls down a gutter in front of yellow fruit-stand flaps
This makes me ache for something
and possibly what I ache for is you
but it is just as possible that what I ache for
even though it's only March, is lemonade

from *Contemporary Verse 2*

STEVEN HEIGHTON ❧

In Order to Burn

In a sleeping pill season, in a REM-stage remission,
revisit a curve in a certain cold river

where the birches are in full business
and the grass of the banks is wild mint.

It's years, yet you're both stretched out here still,
rib to rib, hearts happily talking over each other,

and above you somehow the same southerlies,
same sunfish school of pewter leaves

pulsing in ultramarine. Remembrance:
how every touch and utterance

seemed tender calamity, so even now,
in the locked-in stasis of this sedation,

the couple you made is still current
on that earth. You were conscious, then,

even sleeping, and what's wholly lived keeps looping
through some unforgetting amnion, so pulse

to pulse, fully personed, you return. (Not that she can—
yet see how, even now, she is nowhere else.)

from *PRISM*

JASON HEROUX ❧

Allowance

After I finished my chores
I was given a raindrop
to spend in the woods,
I was given a shadow
to spend in the light.
A hook to spend
in the fish, a tank
to spend in the war,
a bird to spend
in the cage, a shiver
to spend in the wind.

from *Branch*

GERALD HILL ❧

Why We Don't Know

Trams slow
tracks curve or taxis
block the rails. Maybe we're the ones

curving. Get to the end
we hop off. All day
we don't know and it rains we walk

with canes for umbrellas. Maybe it's
the wine we're about to drink two euros
a bottle. Mornings we catch

BBC World Service. Pakistan will never know
Kashmir again. We lay out our streets in
a grid after earthquakes. The trams

move slow or topple. We start a page
and down the hill turn it filling
the square like birds

hopping on tables. Meet
the quake of '14 though
nothing yet has fallen.

Lisbon, Jan.28, 2014

from *Canadian Literature*

by the time he hit the floor

and his cigarette still burning on the striproom table
beside a can of worms.

He would've been leaning there that morning
in the barn, near the radio, after ploughing the fields, before
heading for Caledonia to fish on the Grand

had three-four good years after his first heart attack, see
but he'd taken it up again, lost all that nice pink from his face,
turned grey.

Vincent Church was visiting from Waterford
—oh, they liked to talk about swap, and fixing things, you know
Vince found him, and never recovered from the sight, our neighbour

Koslowski called the ambulance, took him straight to the funeral home
and went to tell Mother and Margaret at St. Bernard's.

I was in Niagara with my girl after Ray Rutherford's wedding,
we drove down there from Meaford, it was early May
our last blossom days

the start of tough slogging,
a hard summer with all that had to be done, you know
during tobacco harvest.

I'd kept six hives of bees but they swarmed
late in the season because I hadn't got the supers on
and I felt so bad about that, they wouldn't likely survive.

You remember the rhyme, *a swarm in May is worth a load of hay in June a silver spoon, but a swarm in July's not worth a fly.*

It was August already, I was driving boat
bringing loads of tobacco from the field, dreaming of Regina

when the sky went dim, a black veil, my bees
and I couldn't stop to tend them.

That's when I knew I couldn't do everything, I'd failed, see
it was all blow-sand knolls and wet spots
and watching my bees fly away.

Tobacco still ripening in the fields when it came time
to leave for school in Toronto, Mother made me a bread pudding

and a pact that I'd not come home 'til Thanksgiving.
Somehow she'd get the crops in, and she sat at the table
weeping, sweet steam beading the plate, the tears

filled my throat like lit sumac and honeycomb, beekeeper's smoke.
She'd made my favourite dessert, and you know
I couldn't touch it.

—as told by my father

from *Arc Poetry Magazine*

Wing On

for James Schuyler

What pebbles to place on your tomb
hold all through your jazz memorial

in the Wing On funeral home
A row of bluets to stain the stone

Just one greasy lipstick kiss on your granite
in a ruby shade called *Willing*

not smeared like Oscar Wilde's marble tomb
Set delphinium feathers and Noxzema jars

pill bottles filled with catalogue seeds
a tiny plastic boat to swim out to

It's pink-shirted teenagers day up the street
Honk for Equal Love they wave

Let's flashmob the grotto at Lourdes
Let's fishnet the legs of all the girls

Amaryllis, hyacinth, every shade of rosehip
a cross-stitched border of spruce and juniper

Scoop a few coins into the busker's cup
And buy the poet a meal

Why don't we take a yellow song, carefree
and refined, put it on a long stem and stand it

in a tall skinny crystal vase? Add a pair
of topsiders to wear on the little boat

from *The Malahat Review*

SALLY ITO ❧

Idle

in the pew as in life, awaiting deliverance from this dullness
that is all exhort and exhaust; where O Salvation art thou?
Sometimes it comes in fist-cherub face of the bawling infant's
cacophonous interruption, crow squawk to the sermon song,
insisting on milk and crumbs in the ever-present *Now*—
that is your idle alertness. Waiting, it seems, is a ponderous affair
and you have no time for it, this idleness that is the only state
that permits of dream, scheme, and imagine. And yet,
you are nonetheless here in the pew, attending the urge to
connect with world's soul weathers, its weal and woe
sometimes your own, you must admit. You are that car in park,
idling, engine humming, nowhere to go and that is as it should be,
you chastise yourself, squirming and ungrateful in your praise.

from *Prairie Fire*

Engraving

Between the whinging devil and the menacing old man,
and through the night that insofar as we know began
before we did, and will, like Borges's knight, succeed us;
companioned by the horse and dog, and armoured to the teeth
(the helmet, under which the golden hair is all piled up,
and breastplate to conceal, here, not her sex so much as her little child):

this is the way the ladies ride,
this is the way the ladies ride,
this is the way the ladies ride.

from *Partisan*

Late Changes in the Homescape

The dog, a whole summer spent
variously announcing his age
in chronic pant and geezer snore
wild, blind blunders off porch and stair
days ensnared by sprinkler,
night by wily phone cord.

The barn, once our dodgy gymnasium.
Hay-chute luge, short but deadly steep.
Chicken-house leap, similarly wicked.
Dad's little workshop off the back
and upstairs the growing stacks
of sleepy broken things.

All times tethered to ones undone.
The barn hulking in sight
of a dozen newer distractions,
the dog pushed from lap,
now quietly panting at the garden—
utterly baffled, forever game.

from *The Fiddlehead*

A Little Advice from the Matriarch

1
If you want to see far,
turn your back on the sun.

Don't look for the road you are walking on.

2
Knock at your door.
That was your self you were talking to.

Politeness can't hurt.

3
Don't shout at the ox!
You must care for it.

4
I had no name when I came in.
Today I can't remember it.

5
Jonah had no line, no hook.
Imagination coughed him up.

He didn't want to tell anyone.

6
Don't hold your nose while passing God.
A letter has been sent to you.

7
Valley or peak?
Same sky!

8
Stop sitting around!
Have you nothing to do?

from *Literary Review of Canada*

JEFF LATOSIK ❧

The Internet

I first heard about it in a Burger King.
Its aims seemed as elusive as the stock ticker
or why some people stayed in marriages.
The future was flying cars, phone screens, and Minidisc.
I bused tables with a cloth that mucked the laminate sheen
and, just that Spring, an annular eclipse ringed the sky
like we were suddenly looking down a cabled conduit.

Then, as if an indigenous strain moving beyond a range map,
people started *getting* it, birdsong calling up from basements,
the pink noise, hiss, and crackle of a connection made.
And somebody already had some pictures: the body,
pixelated, bare, with the feeling you were overseeing it,
moving along the conveyer belt of banner ads.
Days went by like they were being dragged into a bin.

Somewhere, fibres tethered us to a warehouse or a factory,
but for them the feed seemed as ephemeral as a thought.
The search bar like a mail slot you could lift
just enough to see inside somebody else's space.
It wasn't a place, but you could go there.
At night, blinds down, but windows open, flags of light
were quietly raised from main floors up into our rooms.

from *The Puritan*

Mid-Autumn Festival

In August you bought a box of moon cakes
and ate every last one by yourself.
Even kept the beribboned gift bag
for yourself. You refused to remember

the traditions, to honour the ritual
of sharing these symbols of family unity
and togetherness. The cakes sat
in your belly like cakes of soap

or packed mud, so dense and heavy they hurt—
the salted egg yolk crumbling between
your teeth, the grit of seeds and nuts
and chunks of sugared melon, the furrowed

pastry stamped with calligraphy
you never learned to read. Maybe this
was compensation for something that drifted
out of reach your entire childhood ...

But even if *love* was never said,
even if they called you *fat little pig*,
they kept nothing for themselves.
Drank mug after mug of hot water

to trick their stomachs into fullness
while feeding you mounds of rice
piled with pork and pickled vegetables,
bowls of congee studded with century egg,

pastries swollen with red bean and lotus seed.
You were a monster: hungry all the time
and furious, squeezing slices of Wonderbread
and gobs of margarine into raw yellow balls

you shoved into your mouth, sobbing.
It was worse than hunger, said the Japanese monks
in training, worse than the beatings—
those weeks when they trekked into the cities

to beg and were forced to eat every morsel
heaped into their copper bowls. The pain
of satiation worse than the windy emptiness
howling through their bellies the rest of the year.

from *Ricepaper*

An Ecology of Being and Non-Being

Yesterday, the first day of spring. Today, large flakes of snow flutter in the absence of wind, drop like ghosts of heavy, wet-winged moths from another world. But there is only this world. No need to grieve.

Look at the chickadees in their black caps, huddled in the spruce tree in the southwest corner of the yard. Listen to the starlings raising a racket in the cottonwood across the street. Take up your walking stick, pull on your boots, and meditate that way—one foot after another. Stop wishing for the sky to clear, better to clear your mind with walking and breathing—into the open fields, winter stubble and ice cracking beneath your feet, sun a half-remembered dream, possible only in another season.

Being is straightforward: Before you is the field. Behind you is the village where you live. Geese in the distance eating seed. Coyotes hunting geese. Trees and songbirds. Snow on the brim of your hat. Red tail of a fox disappearing into earth. Breath drifting in clouds, up to where no spirits are gathered. Ten thousand thoughts rising from, descending to, the void. Simple.

Return to your small house. Light a fire. Make an offering of tobacco. Burn sweetgrass. The smoke will rise to the rafters of the sky and beyond. Listen to the dogs yelping at two doves hunkered down on the power line. Warm a bowl of soup and eat. Let your home harbour idleness, some peace, a brief respite from the habitual traps of mind.

But then, there's memory. That old ache in the knee. Your father. Your friends. Aunts and uncles and cousins. All the holes you have dug in your heart to bury your dead.

But here's another memory: You stand in the new-moon night—among Ponderosa pine on a mountainside, half a mile above Okanagan Lake, twenty paces from the retreat house—watching the Perseid meteor shower. The falling lights strip you bare of thought, strip you bare of yourself.

March. Try to remember:
For today, there is no need to grieve.

When spring finally arrives, by its own path and in its own time, take to the backyard, try to nurture something like simplicity: Lupine, coneflowers, bergamot, and wild roses. Chokecherries, crab apples, currants, and plums. Rearrange the rocks you have dragged home from the shoreline of Buffalo Pound, the way you rearranged your thoughts, endlessly, in the long hours and days of winter darkness.

At nightfall, when you come tired to your bed, leave your *self* outside among rocks and roots. There will be sleep. There will be dreams—of a winter yet to come. Fallen seeds. The remnants of clinging fruit to feed the remaining birds.

from *The Puritan*

Rosa Parks

The day her body was laid out for viewing,
I was getting nothing useful done, so I left
work early and drove downtown.
The line of people wound all around
the Museum of African-American History.
I wouldn't get to see her: the wait
would be hours, I'd brought no coins
to feed a meter, and there was nowhere
else to park. A man approached
to offer me all the change in his pockets.
I'll always have fond memories of Detroit.

from *Arc Poetry Magazine*

Balancing Books

Interest in audited financial statements paid by poets
in increments of time's slippage
searching truth
can be expensive
sometimes truth slips
slippage has a shelf life of twenty-two seconds
which when divided by the ability to save
debits attention

breaks interest
being broke I am unable to pay attention
attention deficit is a disorder
for which there is no financial cure.

A poet's financial projections
wiggle between attention to moments
of fanciful flight and numbers dancing
misunderstood overtop monetary vowels
debiting clarity
and threatening loss.

from *The Puritan*

I Run With You Still

I run with you still, across the wet-stuck printed ghosts on pavement,
through rococo swirls of leaves;
inhale exhale inhale out.

I can hear your voice, your chemo-poet timbre of logic—
I've no right to be angry;
I'm a fluid-air-sifted oxy-mitochondrial gambit of enzymes.

And what am I to do with that? To hear you tell it,
you and I were nothing more than protein-infected accidents
who crossed on a trapeze through space-time.

I know we ran barefoot at China Beach, splashing the waves
and the broken shells that whispered up and through the sand,
shadow of an eagle curling on chunks of driftwood pupil black.

But mostly our runs were more quotidian, evening races
along neighbourhood streets and alleys, sweat and limbs and lunging breath
tuned to air and sun and the universe inflating.

Our last run was Big Cedar, beyond Waterman's Variety,
puffing lanes along the lake past tennis courts
and sun-burnt cottages cribbed inside fieldstone fences.

Night was curtaining the water as we turned the corner toward Duffy's,
the pink neon with the half-dead B blinking that intermittent
'ar we always thought suited poor Duffy.

He never bothered to have it fixed anyway;
just stood there tapping ale behind the backwards neon,
dripping axioms like a leaky spigot.

Blue magic racing down-slope toward the shore,
last light kissing the tips of the waves,
midges, and birdsong in the trees; but then a stumble.

You brushed it off, but you were labouring now; I could see the effort,
the pain it cost to plant one foot in front of the other,
one foot in front of the other, over and over again.

Down the lane by the pump house you had to stop and retch
in the rot of rank algae. After you caught your breath you pointed to the
bob and dip of tufted ducks dabbling in a relish of butts and foam,

turds and safes—*There's more than a piece of us in all of that,*
you said, not shamed, not proud, but only a final clear-eyed observation,
a carbon fingernail scratched across the record.

Because I knew you, I knew there'd be no special goodbyes, no embrace,
just the usual *Thanks for the run* and quick handshake. But looking back,
I like to think you gripped my hand a little tighter that day.

I hear you now whenever I run—
the airy gasp and gulp, the cough and spit, the laugh and joke;
the heartbeat of your soles ka-thump ka-thump on the lonely asphalt.

from *The New Quarterly*

CASSIDY MCFADZEAN ❧

Nymph

Forest's pine needles made a false floor
that broke away below me, earth

loosening around the tree's roots
and the rotting log's hollow chambers.

I fell ass-first in the dappled brook
grasping moss-covered rocks,

and scrambled uphill as twigs cut gashes
on my legs, two thin lacerations stinging

with thistles' kisses. To stop myself
from slipping into a nearby fox den,

I fingered half a sheep's skull, purple collagen
hardened to its ridged teeth and skimmed

my hand against a lichen-covered trunk.
It was a smooth rail that pulled me upright.

I held tightly to snapping branches
as maggots writhed, then vanished.

Suspended between certain dirt
and a glossy cobweb caught at head height,

the tree's outstretched digit caught hold
of my ring and wedded itself to me.

from *The Walrus*

DAVID MCGIMPSEY

**When Sylvia Plath said 'People or stars regard me sadly' I think she
mostly meant 'people'**

Poetry's not hard. All you have to do is,
instead of saying things like "I washed my clothes
at a motel laundromat in Orchard Park,
NY," say "I ate gold in Milan."

Tell it slant. You don't have to use old-fashioned
phrases like "Write down Prince John a villain!"
Just imagine you're at a seminar
with Prince John, making fun of fat people.

Show don't tell. Saying "my feelings were hurt
when you winced at my Burger King jokes"
is very *telling.* Saying "You have great taste
in movies!" *shows* us more with fewer words.

Make it new. You learn from the old masters,
taking, say, Keats's "I believe you had
liked me for my own sake" and updating it
as "Can I be on your panel at AWP?"

from *Literary Review of Canada*

STEVE MCORMOND ❧

All-Inclusive

Up the beach from the supper club's sprawling
patio where beleaguered servers thread the crowd,
bearing trays of watered-down Cuba Libres,
grilled mahi-mahi on skewers, near the striped
changing huts and sea kayaks on steel racks,
two men pace figure eights in the sand, their faces
lit by cellphone screens. One sports a loud
shirt and a fresh sunburn, the other, darker
skinned, wears a once-white apron and hairnet.
They circle, pivoting on sandaled heels.
It's a kind of wary dance, the boundaries
invisible, yet mutually agreed. The elusive green
bars were here yesterday. There's always something
that can't wait: a friend's birthday, a baby overdue,
someone in a nursing home, a child to wish goodnight
before the sitter switches out the light; niggles, logistics,
some little piece of news. The odd couple
commiserates silently—the one who chafes
at his leisure, the other on a smoke break.
What they have to say won't stay bottled up;
what they want to hear is the one thing
that will permit them sleep. But the satellites
won't cooperate: the night air carries
only the surf's white noise, merengue
from the resort casino on the next point.
It's an old story: figures on a far shore,
hands raised to the sky, searching for a signal.
Two tiny lights like fireflies engulfed by dark
inhuman scenery. The drone of scouring waves,
the moon stirring the iron filings of the sea.

from *Lemon Hound*

The Clock

The clock began to tick. Or I began
to hear it in the room where it had always
ticked and I had rested. The rhythm

appeared, like blood that had been there
circling invisible that surges from some cut,
that bursts open a flaw. A spurt, another,

regular. Won't they ever end? Won't it run out?
And it keeps running out, the blood in the terrified
attention fastened on the fountain. The drops

fall on the floor, gather, and flow out of sight
to harden somewhere, lose the nature of blood,
be knowable as blood to the scientist only

who comes later, tests the dust
and says at the end of scrutiny, This is blood.
The motionless face of the clock had begun

to forge forward, in that room that long had held
my body lying still. It was speaking now
a rhythm that ought to underlie a song. A rhythm

made by the mind's arithmetic, as it figured ways
the skein of featureless ticks could be arranged:
iamb and trochee, spondee, dactyl, amphimacer,

all the paeans... A rhythm that made my breath stop
with conviction the next tick wasn't coming. Star systems
were conceived and died in the silences

between each two. "Unbearable suspense," it's called:
the heart expecting to recognize it's dead,
it's been dead while the brain had to wait

a further second—the length of all true thoughts—
for the blood's stoppage to reach it. Impossible, that ticking.
It can't exist. In my room, in the resting of my body

there was no time, no future for any new sound
to come from or to sound in. All was silence.
And yet the ticking had come. So all was now

a prow moving in a sea
of black places that were not
till it cut into them. The voice of the clock

went on that way in my craw, dragging me
between excitement and exhaustion
while I longed to be left alone, to be restored

to the quiet of before, where I was paused
permanently, to consider until I could grasp it
this being underway.

from *NewPoetry*

HOA NGUYEN ❧

From the Autobiography of Malcolm X

Anyway, now, each day I live
as if I am already dead

and I tell you what I would like
for you to do. When I am dead

I say it that way because
from the things I know

I do not expect to live
long enough to read this book

in its finished form—
I want you to just watch and

see if I'm not right in what
I say: that the white man

in his press
is going to identify me

with "hate"

from *The Capilano Review*

The Exile's Home Gallery

One ancient bayside city in a balmy palette:
peach façades, a fuchsia door,
boys flipping open a creel.
Five shirts take their ease on a jigging clothesline,
white sleeves buoyant and secure.

Virgil was schooled here,
just beyond this etching.
How hard, the next pastel suggests, to leave any city
that invented opera buffa,
not to mention the mandolin.

Three hallway maps immortalize
hamlets in baroque fonts.
Trees neat as a row of asterisks
fleck a diagrammed bosque.
Mountains look cozy as tents

ringing another town, settled in shuttles
of Celts, Slavs, Germans—
Paleo-trench to *oppidum* to stockade;
its Bohemia became renowned
as a magicians' haven.

But Nero summered in one city,
shelling unroofed two more;
that bosque gardener's son
couldn't rise (and who even thought of
the mapmaker's daughter?),

coins weren't worth bottlecaps,
plague deployed rat-tailed crews,
farms shrivelled with famine, and streets
where prayer-shawls had fluttered three hundred years
were cleared of Jews.

Just one painting by an amateur:
pads of cumuli;
heeling on cobalt waves, a brown skiff.
Those watching it tilt, weeping,
can't catch the voyager's eye—

a girl in black—thin arms—
gazes toward no sign of land.
Her face is turned away;
she grips a jolting tiller
in her too-small hand.

from *Partisan*

MATT RADER ❧

Mavis Gallant

for Elizabeth Bachinsky, with a line from Maggie Nelson

All our poems now are for people we know
And our babies. It's 1846. In the North
Charitable Infirmary the musical society plays
"The Bells of Shandon" for the women of Cork
Who are so hungry their bellies recall
Those late days of pregnancy. "Men bore me,
Especially Great Men," is what I wish
I'd said to a woman I was trying to love once
With books and fucking. But all I know
About books and fucking is that they change
And I'm tired of men going on about men.
If loneliness is solitude with a problem.
If I'm scared alonely. What did they do
With all those babies and people we knew?

from *The Walrus*

Good Measure

We left this house, the dog, the garden.
We broke the vows, the hearth, the marriage.
We left behind for good measure
dust, debt, sediment. Left the ash,
the keys, cushions to the futon
in the crawl space. A cracked tank
emptied of fish. We left
discards at the curb. Left the fights,
the separate beds, the separate loves, the place
our daughter learned to walk
and run.

We left this house. We left
the built-in vacuum, the neighbor's leaf blower
a man who edged his lawn with scissors. We left
the picket fence, white lilac. Left
a double-wide garage, a stack of bricks
fire with a switch left off.
The years left lines upon our faces.

Each false start, ash of the dog under bleeding hearts.
Poppies, orange and gold. A stack of textbooks.
Those years blew through us. You took a hit of sadness
blew smoke in my mouth. I held it in
until I saw stars.

There was a fire, dog's grit and bone, cold tea
in a cold mug, gold ring returned.
We left a forwarding address
pencil marks in the doorframe:
the height they were at different times
though we'd stopped growing long since.

from *The Fiddlehead*

ARMAND GARNET RUFFO ❧

Sacred Beaver, 1969

Nothing you see is ever what you think it is.
The surface of things reflected in a lake.

You see Ahmik, beaver, hauling a branch
Busy at work preparing for winter.

You see a rock painting as you paddle past.
For you there is nothing between the two.

Then you are in your grandfather's voice
He is sharing one of his stories with you.

About long ago when giant beaver roamed
The Lake Nipigon area of Great Turtle Island.

One day a Thunderbird grabbed Ahmik
And lifted the squirming creature up into the sky.

And struggle as it might the beaver could not escape
Thunderbird's yellow talon hooks.

The more it sought to free itself the more
Its gashes opened and bled upon the earth below.

So that all the red ochre we see today
Used by shaman-artists of old

It is all really beaver blood.
All really about here plunged into you like a stake.

Norval Morrisseau's grandfather Potan Nanakonagos told him many stories that connect the world of animals to the world of humans. Much of Morrisseau's work speaks of this relationship and about our inseparable interdependence to all living creatures.

from *Arc Poetry Magazine*

Mosquitoes, Scissors, Stars

Warm nights, we'd gather on the front lawn, naked
        Except for Speedos. As the first stars appeared over

Silver Heights, we'd dash through the sprinkler & then stand, frozen,
        Arms stretched out to the side, our legs

Open like scissors. The one boy who could
        Stand there the longest, without moving, without

Flinching, not even an eyelid, while squadrons
        Of mosquitoes bit him, would win. I remember

Looking aside, without moving my head, & seeing
        The mosquitoes' tiny, transparent sacs, all over

My arms, fill with blood. I remember turning red
        With welts, & walking to the house, victorious. My mother

Thought I had the measles. The fevered whine
        Around my ears, then, had been a whine

Of the purest moment, a moment that would
        Carry me through childhood & remain forever the music

Of a small, painful ecstasy, where, as the word
        Dictates, I was outside of myself, looking back at whoever

I thought I was, or would become, or would fail
        To become. And I remember, too, clearly,

As the scent of lilac drifted in through an opened
        Window, pulling crisp sheets down on the bed,

Another sound, which was a kind of music
        As well, but deeper, eerily deeper, that widened

And darkened the night beyond those stars
      Into a blackness that deepened more of itself, & then more, until

The sheerest film of it produced a dubious gift:
      It flowed out of a throat at the other end

Of the house, a throat no longer belonging
      To my mother, but impersonating hers,

Forging madly past words,
      Toward the unsayable—a long, low

Nightly groan against Existence, which, for her
      Must have been as unjustifiable as the stars.

from *Prairie Fire*

KILBY SMITH-MCGREGOR ❧

Wake Up Remembering Oranges

Wake up remembering oranges and I
curl, count to ten, roll off your sister's cot,
compose a list of things we need to buy.

You're in her kitchen, with that insurance guy
I guess, but I can't face you, this, my nerves are shot.
Wake up remembering oranges and I

slink upstairs, root out the weed I know is there, get high,
rediscover the reasons I stopped smoking pot,
compose a list of things we need to buy

to start again, like toothpaste, a new house, try
to conceive of combusting in flame—not
waking up remembering oranges, and I

try singeing a little hair, daring myself to cry.
What's burned can be bought, learned. I can be taught.
Compose a list of things we need to buy.

Remembering oranges, not gas left on. To lie
a little—easier than I thought. The shock
of waking up.
                Remembering oranges, I
compose a list of things we need to buy.

from *The Malahat Review*

Forty

for D

It was a black-and-white episode,
our stroll along the shore road at

Tobermory. Sodium lamps did the best
they could for us in their limited spectrum

and reach, walked us out to the end of the dock,
made a short-armed gesture to the total dark.

You posed on a cache of traps. Seamlessly,
we integrated with the background.

It had been quiz night in the Mishnish Pub,
the river bordering Zambia on the tip of our tongues,

rugby, as ever, an unknown quantity, like the Latin name
for onion. We couldn't pick Lily Cole out of a lineup

if she'd robbed us at knifepoint, and now couldn't see
through to the limits of our sight. A constellation

of pale boats emerged floating on the air, the horizon
had closed its eyes and disappeared. In this,

our own were not deceived, it's the mind that makes
inferences. When lying in a small room in the dark,

you often travel distances in a kind of daylight,
don't you. You left me sleeping

and went back out to the seawall, the drifting
boats, each a new month awaiting your captaincy.

In the cell water, eye water, the water thought
floats on, rigging clanking softly in the breeze

and afterbreeze, you were anchored
by unseen lines to the harbour.

from *Brick*

JOHN STEFFLER ❧

I Haven't Looked at These in Years

my beloved father was human, here's his hand holding
his knife, it's how I still remember him, I laid the knife
under his hand and covered him, my beloved sister
was human, mine were the last fingers to touch hers,
I placed this needle—it looks smaller here than it was—
between her finger and thumb, my father used to say
whatever eats leaves waste and hands are hungrier than
mouths, he said human hands are born toothless but
make their own teeth, here I am with my brush, and here
with the camera, beloved brush, the camera I'm not
so sure about, it meant a lot of arguing about catching
god, here you notice I've got it in both hands, very
human, and here I'm holding it in my teeth for a joke,
my father would have hated that, this pipe in my uncle's
mouth, see, my beloved uncle, was always a problem, only
animals carry with their mouths, my beloved father said,
leave the ashes, the scraps, the slash, the bones, we're
made to go forward, he said, that's why we haven't got
eyes in the backs of our heads or toes behind our heels,
here's my beloved aunt holding a pistol, my sickly cousin
with a book, some close-ups, hand with rosary, steering
wheel, telephone, cheese grater, matches, food dish,
beloved shoe, my father said never carry junk, remember
people only if you can describe their hands, them
touching you, some of them, hands want to reach for
what's clean, what's young, he said, what's past is
past, or maybe passed is passed, now, he said, is for
packing up, here he's shutting the trunk of the car

from *The Malahat Review*

Elephant v. Rhinoceros

I. Witnesses

Ctesias, physician
Artemidorus Ephesius, geographer
Diodorus Siculus, historian
Oppian, poet
Pliny, scientist and historian
Valentin Ferdinand, printer
Albrecht Dürer, artist
Guillaume de Salluste du Bartas, poet
Edward Topsell, naturalist
Oliver Goldsmith, novelist
Commodore George Anson
Captain Thomas Williamson

Jean Chardin, traveller
Comte de Buffon, naturalist
John Church, physician
Stephani Polito, menagerist
Richard Owen, anatomist

II. Opening Arguments

The rhinoceros is especially hostile to the elephant
There is a natural antipathy
    a natural enmity between the beasts
The rhinoceros is a natural-born enemy of the elephant
It is the elephant's inveterate
    sworn
    fierce
    deadly
    mortal enemy

No antipathy has been observed between these animals
In captivity, they live quietly together
without offence or provocation

The rhinoceros prepares itself for combat by sharpening its horn against
gets ready for battle by filing its horn on
Before attacking, it sharpens
always first whets its horn upon the stones
against a rock

The rhinoceros attacks
surprises
opens the fight with
overcomes the elephant by

charging it at the chest
thrusting its forehead under the belly
fastening its horn in the lower part of the elephant's belly
In the encounter it strikes the elephant on the chest
runs at the elephant with his head between his forelegs
slips under
goes especially for
strikes most of all at the belly
shoves its horn in the stomach

which it knows to be softer
the softest part
tenderest and most penetrable part
weakest part of the body
thinnest skin
where his sharpened blade will in

As the rhinoceros is naturally of a pacific temper
it is probable that accounts of it engaging the elephant
are without foundation

The rhinoceros rips open the flesh with its horn as a sword
    rips up the elephant's belly
    tears it to pieces
       without mercy
    gores him
    wounds mortally
    opens his guts

The elephant's entrails tumble out

                    The rhinoceros has no taste for flesh

III. Physical Evidence

The elephant is often found dead in the forests pierced
with the horn of a rhinoceros
elephants are occasionally found dead
obviously from wounds given by the rhinoceros

            A rhinoceros dead at the London Zoo
            seventh rib fractured by an elephant
            poking its tusks through the palings
            between their enclosures
            death ascribed to injury of the left lung
            caused by the fracture

IV. Eyewitness Accounts

Lisbon, 1515
Valentin Ferdinand:
On the day of the Blessed Trinity
an elephant was led to a courtyard
near the King's Palace
A rhinoceros was led to the same place
The elephant uneasy and furious

uttered a tremendous cry, ran
to one of the barred windows
wrenched the iron bars
with trunk and teeth
fled away

Persia, 1667
Jean Chardin:
On the left of the Royal stables
were two great elephants
covered with cloths of gold brocade
And one rhinoceros
So near one to the other
the animals showed not the least
aversion or uneasiness

Africa, 1807
Captain Thomas Williamson:
The late Major Lally witnessed
a most desperate engagement
between a rhinoceros
and a large, male elephant
the latter protecting a small herd
retiring in a state of alarm
The elephant was worsted
and fled into heavy jungle

London, 1814
Stephani Polito:
The formidable rhinoceros
one of the largest ever seen
In the adjoining den, in the same apartment
a fine large male elephant
adorned with long ivory tusks
The two animals so closely united
so reconciled
as to take their food from one other

V. Closing Arguments

The rhinoceros kills the elephant
    kills many of them
many a time it lays so mighty a beast dead in the dust

                    unless the rhinoceros is prevented by the trunk and tusks
                    the elephant may defend itself with the trunk or teeth then
                    throw the rhinoceros down
                    throw it on the ground
                    and kill it

                    the elephant succumbing to the pain drops
                    and crushes its enemy
                    by the weight of its body

          seldom does combat cease without death of both fighters

The rhinoceros gores the elephant and carries him off upon his head, but the blood and fat of the elephant run into his eyes, and make him blind; he falls to the ground; and what is very astonishing, the roc carries them both away in her claws, to be meat for her young ones

The Court finds both weight and the weight of the evidence to be on the side of the elephant. The scales of justice tip in its favour.

[Note: Fragments of text borrowed from: Ctesias, *Ancient India*; Diodorus Siculus, *Bibliotheca historica*; Oppian, *Kynegetika*; Pliny, *The Natural History*; Valentin Ferdinand, *Letter*; Guillaume de Salluste du Bartas, *La Semaine*; Jean Chardin, *Travels in Persia*; Edward Topsell, *History of Four-Footed Beasts and Serpents*; *Arabian Nights*; Comte de Buffon, *Natural History*; George Anson, *A Voyage Around the World*; Oliver Goldsmith, *A History of the Earth and Animated Nature*; Thomas Williamson, *Oriental Field Sports*; John Church, *A Cabinet of Quadrupeds*; Richard Owen, *On the Anatomy of the Indian Rhinoceros*.]

    from *The Puritan*

Duffle

It's hard to be at the bus stop
in the pulp-mill fog
with Sue Dawkins the morning after my stepdad put
buckshot in the ass
of her dog for
killing our chickens

so I stand with hands in my ski vest
in the bad breath
of Prince George Pulp and
stare at the buttons of Sue Dawkins's coat
the morning
after her father drove over
and saw by flashlight
the clumps of red feathers
the dog had caused

you were within your rights   do away with

are snippets of what he spoke
like a teacher
slowly
doling out a sad spelling test.
No tilt to his voice except for the
cracking up
at the edge of his words when he saw the
dead lump
the black dog had become.

The two of us
Sue and I
stand on the side of a highway
in cold air that moves only with the whoosh of a Kenworth
and I try not to count the dog hair
that sticks to a blue coat

that is a sort I've never seen before and doesn't come
from Kresge's
wood toggles on it
each one with a leather loop to hold it tight
the morning after my stepdad slurred back at her dad
because he'd been boozing before he got the gun
and said *buckshot in the ass* one more time
because he likes the way it sounds.

from *EVENT*

JOHN TERPSTRA ❦

Vocation

I can see myself lying on my stomach
on the mattress, beneath a sloped bedroom
ceiling, listening to the radio all summer
because I had nothing else to do.

Because I had nothing else to do but
lie on my bed and listen to the radio, for what
seemed like the entire summer vacation,
I developed a comprehensive knowledge
       of the top-forty radio hit songs.

Much of that three-minute music
was forgettable, although I have not forgotten it.
In between were songs that made the wait worthwhile.
And they all shared in that free articulation of feeling.

The free articulation of feeling. How did they do it?
I thought I was bored and had nothing to do.
Meanwhile, the guardian angel of my psyche
kept me pinned to the mattress, mindless and rapt.

    from *Grain*

SOUVANKHAM THAMMAVONGSA ❧

Gayatri

I have a picture of us when we are seven
but we aren't in it. At the time it was taken

we thought we were. We posed with our wide
grins and best-friends-forever certainty. I angled

the camera to capture us in front of a Christmas tree.
All the sparkling tinsel and dangling silver balls aren't there.

There is only the ceiling and the tip
of the pine needle. There isn't a star or an angel

on top. I have kept this picture of us for years,
the only one to remember and laugh at what happened

to us then. It was taken before a time you could
see a picture on a screen, see how it turned out

and decide whether it was worth keeping. I think of you
now and again, the plain peanut butter sandwiches we ate

with apples. You said you were going to be a dentist
when you grew up, and with a fork and a spoon

you determined it was possible I would live
and sent me home with a bag full of Twizzlers and hair bands.

from *The Walrus*

NICK THRAN

Local Weirdos

I do not actually believe that the cows are snickering
in the nearby fields, even though I have left drops
of my own blood on the A-frame floor
after chipping the frozen patties with a knife
and putting the blade into my own hand.
S. careens the car down highway 62, baby blowing
raspberries in the back, tractors and tourists slow
on the road, and me in the front seat bleating—
one quarter in pain and the rest in self-reproach
for having jabbed metal into the fine-tuned machine
of the day: sections for working, sections for caring
for child: balance and poise and elaborate dance
gone to cud with one slip of the handle. S., sure
hand on the wheel, says go easy on yourself,
as though editing the melodrama out of the poem
I am not composing. We don't crash. There's no
lineup at the hospital, where the doctor, steady
as Sunday service, works the thread and needle, says,
"Knew there was a poet in our midst, but to us
he was just another one of the local weirdos."
The nature of cows seems gentler on the calm
drive back. Go easy. I'm all stitched up. Glad
of the baby, of S., of Al, of cows. Of the doctor too.
Time thaws us all. I judge men as harshly as he does.

from *The Fiddlehead*

TARA-MICHELLE ZINIUK ❧

By the Lachine Canal I Sat Down and...

You send me a text that says, "You're hard not to love,"
followed by one that says, "You're hard to love."
One of these things is as true as the other to you.

You keep breaking and breaking up, fixing and fixing up,
breaking this and me, you leave and return. We do.

Split hairs in our throats, wet Y-fronts, sweaty rims of caps.
Hands on bellies and on the absence of bellies and necks.
Hearts flitting and flying and leaving again.

I stand in front of my old apartment, cold, and wonder
how anyone could fall in love in Montreal twice;
text my ex, the only one who is a friend, to ask
if people still cry by the canal, or if everything I know of this town is passé.

Everyone here is having the same conversation about gender as they were a
dozen years ago, the same conversations about black pants.

We don't know how to ask for time, for directions,

A bright blue robin, improbable for the city,
before us, in starts and fits too.

from *Taddle Creek*

JAMES ARTHUR is from Toronto and currently lives in Baltimore. His first book, *Charms Against Lightning*, was published in 2012 by Copper Canyon Press. He has received the Amy Lowell Travelling Poetry Scholarship, a Hodder Fellowship, a Stegner Fellowship, a Discovery/The Nation Prize, and a Fulbright Scholarship to the Seamus Heaney Centre for Poetry. Arthur teaches in the Writing Seminars at Johns Hopkins University.

Arthur writes, "'A Local History' describes what used to be my grandparents' farm, several miles north of Pickering, Ontario. I wrote the poem as an elegy for my grandmother, who died a few years ago at the age of 93; she outlived my grandfather by almost thirty years. I think that 'A Local History' is also about childhood fantasy, about how we remember the dead, how we imagine the dead, and how we imagine the places that we're from, especially once those places are no longer accessible to us. Though I grew up in Toronto, my four-year-old son was born in St. Louis and is growing up in Baltimore. It seems unreal to me that he'll have no memory of his great-grandmother, or of that farm, but in a way all family histories, all local histories, are like that: living memory reaches back for a couple of generations, and then it drops off into the unknown."

JOELLE BARRON lives in Fort Frances, Ontario, with her daughter. She works as a librarian, a school secretary, and a doula. She received her MFA in Creative Writing from the University of British Columbia in 2014. Her work has been published in *The Malahat Review*, *The Dalhousie Review*, *Arc Poetry Magazine*, *The New Quarterly*, and others. She won the Open Season Award for Poetry in 2014.

Of "This Job Ends in Six Months," Barron writes, "I wrote this poem when I was working as a nanny in Vancouver in 2013. I remember being struck by the idea that this child who I cared for on a daily basis, and had come to love, would grow up with no memories of our time together. A couple months in, his parents moved from their basement apartment in Kitsilano to a condo development in New Westminster. Our days together took on a surreal aspect in a neighborhood that didn't know what it was yet; farms, half-built buildings, and ranch-style '70s homes coexisted in a kind of swamp. I wanted the poem to preserve a moment in time that was precious to me, something for both of us to keep."

HUGO BEAUCHEMIN-LACHAPELLE is a poet living in Québec. He teaches at CÉGEP Édouard Montpetit.

ALEXANDER ROCK is from Montréal, where he is a graduate student at the Université de Montréal. He is a co-translator of Louis Patrick Leroux's *Dialogues fantasques pour causeurs éperdues* [False Starts], along with Leroux and Katia Grubisic (Talon Books, forthcoming). Rock's writing has been featured in *The Puritan, Lemonhound,* and *Matrix* and he has also modestly worked as a playwright and dramaturge in productions of Joanna Baillie's *Witchcraft* and Leroux's *Milford Haven.*

Rock writes, "I worked on this poem as part of a collection of translations for *The Puritan*'s special summer supplement 'À la prochaine fois: 1995 and Literature in Post-Referendum Québec.' Though I had worked on some translations in the past, I felt out of touch with my Québecois peers and so was compelled to first do some homework. I knew that I wanted to work on something written by someone under the age of 40 and composed within the last few years, no earlier than the protests of 2012. I also wanted to find something that was political in tone and content and that reflected the concerns of contemporary Québec; that is, something that would speak to the pervasive mood of disenfranchisement across the province, and indeed, all over the continent. Operating on a writer's budget, I opted to sneak from one bookstore to the next and leaf through countless collections taking photos of the poems that hit all of the right notes. This is how I discovered Catherine Dorion and Jean-Philippe Dupuis, poets whose indignation matched my own. I then found Hugo Beauchemin-Lachapelle's work on *poemsale.com*, a French-language website devoted to publishing poetry that is 'dirty, bloodied, and tattered' and that offers a platform for poets who find themselves on the periphery of the literary establishment. Beauchemin-Lachapelle's 'Sans-titre' contained everything that I had been looking for and, what's more, was austere, sardonic, and terse. It was, in short, a marriage made in the gutter."

ANDREA BENNETT, from Dundas, Ontario, is a National Magazine Award-winning writer whose work has been published by *The Atlantic, The Walrus, Geist, Grain, Hazlitt, Lemon Hound,* and others. She's the associate editor of *Maisonneuve,* and the author of the poetry book *Canoodlers* (Nightwood, 2014).

Of "Northern Rockies," bennett writes, "In summer 2014, with the support of an Access Copyright grant, I travelled up to northeastern British Columbia to interview people about fracking, the resource economy, land as livelihood, and a dispute that had occurred between a local environmentalist and a town's mayor. Staying in hotels was expensive, so I camped out in RV parks. It was an amazing and memorable experience—I loved it up there. But I was also struck by the fact of having grown up in a small town, and returning to another one where I was an outsider, a very visible outsider ('If you want to talk further, I'm in the blue and yellow tent at Triple G Hideaway!'), and also there to ask some potentially uncomfortable questions. I had a couple moments of vertigo, the plane of small-town past converging with the plane of small-town present; meanwhile, my RV park neighbours changed nightly, and I knew I'd soon be passing through, too."

SHERI BENNING grew up on a farm in Saskatchewan. She's published three books of poetry: *The Season's Vagrant Light: New and Selected Poems* (Carcanet Press), *Thin Moon Psalm* (Brick Books) and *Earth After Rain* (Thistledown Press). Her poetry, short fiction, and essays have appeared in numerous Canadian, British, and Irish journals and anthologies. Benning completed a PhD at the University of Glasgow and is currently a postdoctoral fellow at the University of Regina.

Benning writes, "Early December, many years ago, I dropped everything and flew across the country to visit my best friend and her new baby. I'd been having one of those terrible spells—it seemed that no matter which direction I turned I was met with grief. 'Come, stay with me,' my best friend said. I packed my bags. That Christmas season, we spent our days delighting in the baby and our evenings feasting on food and each other's company. I read a book of essays about walking in Paris. It snowed everyday. We curled up together on her red couch and between nursing my best friend napped, her head in my lap, the baby in her arms. Hope after hope is lost, the deeper comfort that can be found after sadness is endured, those plain moments of intimacy that sate us—this is what I was thinking about when I wrote 'Vigil.'"

TIM BOWLING lives in Edmonton and is the author of thirteen poetry collections, five novels, and two works of non-fiction. His work has earned him two Governor General's Award nominations, two Canadian Authors Association Awards, two Writers' Trust of Canada nominations, a Plantos-Acorn Peoples' Poetry Award, five Alberta Book Awards, and a Guggenheim fellowship. His new collection, *The Duende of Tetherball*, will appear in October.

Bowling writes, "Early on, my idyllic childhood along the banks of the Fraser River taught me that life is wonderful. Later, the history of the human species and a growing awareness of mortality put a darker edge to the wonder. Now I'm like many middle-aged people: buffeted between delight and despair, hoping for the best, pushing my little paper boat against the ceaseless current. 'Tetherball' combines images of childhood, the history of the individual's fight against ruthless power systems, and an unyielding admiration for the will to fight against injustice to raise a kind of rallying cry for the spirit. The world often tells us to give in and conform; the tetherball out there in the maelstrom of history tells us the opposite. Year by year, I pay greater attention to what my childhood self tells me, and my poems hear what I see."

JULIE BRUCK is a Montreal native and has lived in San Francisco since 1997. Her third collection, *Monkey Ranch* (Brick Books, 2012), won the Governor General's Award for Poetry. "Flipped" comes from a newly completed manuscript, and other recent poems have appeared in *Hazlitt, Newpoetry.ca, Plume, The Rusty Toque*, and the Academy of American Poets' Poem-a-Day.

Of "Flipped," Bruck writes, "When my daughter was little, she started taking pictures of objects she had loved and outgrown, in order to pass them on to others without feeling like she was losing parts of herself. At six and seven years old, she was making her own *aide-memoire*. This poem shadow boxes with similar fears: what use is an *aide-memoire* when all memory is lost? Perhaps life, and the memory of it, does reside in that toy or dress or house, after all? The poem, like the child, gathers images as a hedge against loss."

SUZANNE BUFFAM is the author of three collections of poetry, *Past Imperfect, The Irrationalist*, and *A Pillow Book*, all with House of Anansi Press. Born and raised in Canada, she lives in Chicago.

Buffam writes, "Over the years I have held various job titles, some of which, if not glamorous, were possessed of a certain lyricism. Part-time Flyer Distributor. Tabulating Machine Operator. Ghost Writer. Visiting Adjunct Artist-in-Residence without Rank. At the time of writing 'Dream Jobs,' however, I did not have a job title. This poem, like the dozens of other lists included in *A Pillow Book*, was written during my infant daughter's naps."

DANI COUTURE was raised on four Canadian military bases and currently lives in Toronto. She is the author of *Good Meat* (Pedlar Press, 2006), *Sweet* (Pedlar Press, 2010), *Yaw* (Mansfield Press, 2014), and the novel *Algoma* (Invisible Publishing, 2011). *Sweet* was shortlisted for the Trillium Book Award for Poetry and won the ReLit Award for poetry. In 2011, Couture received an Honour of Distinction from The Writers' Trust of Canada's Dayne Ogilvie Prize for Emerging LGBT Writers.

Couture writes, "'Black Sea Nettle' is a consideration of the joke 'I don't trust anything that bleeds for five days and doesn't die,' which was first said to me as a teenager. While the line was the starting point for the piece, it is, as its delivery often intends, the final word. What precedes it is consideration of the female body, menstrual cycle (meanings of its presence and absence), blood, and codes of fertility and desire."

LYNN CROSBIE was born in Montreal and is a cultural critic, author, and poet. A PhD in English literature with a background in visual studies, she teaches at the University of Toronto and the Art Gallery of Ontario. Her books include *Pearl, Queen Rat, Life Is About Losing Everything*, and the 2016 Trillium Book Award-nominated *Where Did You Sleep Last Night*. She is a contributing editor at *Fashion*, and a National Magazine Award Winner who has written about sports, style, art, and music.

On "Modestine" in a *poetryinvoice.com* interview Crosbie says, "the poem was inspired by my brother reading Robert Louis Stevenson to my father, and to me, in the hospital. He read it so well, and my dad and I were transfixed. Essentially, it is a poem about a poem."

KAYLA CZAGA is the author of *For Your Safety Please Hold On*, which won The Gerald Lampert Memorial Award and was nominated for The Dorothy Livesay Poetry Prize, and The Governor General's Award for Poetry. Her chapbook, *Enemy of the People*, which explores the Soviet Union under Stalin, was released in Fall of 2015 by Anstruther Press. She lives in Vancouver, where she recently earned an MFA from UBC, and works in a bar.

Of "LIVEJOURNAL.COM/LONELYRADIO," Czaga writes, "While most of my friends had home access to the Internet in elementary school, my family didn't 'plug in' until I was an adolescent. I went through puberty alongside learning how to navigate the Internet, which felt super magical and terrifying. It simultaneously gave me access to enriching people and resources while heightening the sense of sexual menace I faced as a young woman. In the same afternoon, I could collaborate with my friends in Michigan on a sci-fi drama, learn better ways of enacting and hiding self harm, and be asked to show my breasts to a stranger. In the poem, I used the second person in order to evoke the anonymous collective I believed the Internet to be. Sometimes the poem is addressing the speaker who is the 'you.' In other places, the speaker is 'I,' addressing a Lonely Radio who is the 'you'/other. On the Internet, I could interact with people without the feeling that they would hold what I said against me in my daily life. So, I adopted various personas. I experimented in ways that were sometimes damaging and sometimes deeply affirming."

DOROTHY FIELD was born in New York City and immigrated to Canada in 1971. She lives in Victoria in an old house surrounded by berries and fruit trees. She is the author of three books of poetry, the most recent being *The Blackbird Must Be* (Sono Nis, 2010). She is a visual artist as well as a writer, working primarily with printmaking and collage. Before that, she worked with handmade paper and wrote on paper's uses in Asia to connect with the gods.

Of "The Geography of Memory," Field writes, "My mother just turned 97. She still doesn't forget. My father, an irascible man, left after 49 years of marriage for a woman who'd jilted him 50 years before. My mother then had 12 years, probably the best of her life, with a kind and gentle man, and she softened. Numerous trips to Nepal and India may have provided my toughest, truest mothering—something about the grit and the beauty, being confronted with life's precious transience, its desperate immediacy, and its ever-so-sweet surprises. Thus, I try to remember to really taste the raspberries, really smell the February daphne scenting the just-spring air."

KIM FU was born in Calgary, spent most of her life in Vancouver and Montreal, and now lives in Seattle. Her first poetry collection is *How Festive the Ambulance* (Nightwood, 2016). Her debut novel *For Today I Am a Boy* (HarperCollins, 2014) won the Edmund White Award for Debut Fiction, and was a finalist for the PEN/Hemingway Award, a Lambda Literary Award, and the Kobo Emerging Writer Prize, among others.

Of "Lifecycle of the Mole Woman: Infancy as a Human," Fu writes, "This is the first poem in a cycle that tells the story of a woman who goes to live among the mole people. In later poems, she has her eyes gouged out by her mole-prince husband and commiserates with a mermaid—thus the long, incongruous title. 'Infancy' is about the human girlhood that drives her to the mole kingdom in the first place, one haunted by the same limited images of beauty and romance over and over again, as though they were all filmed and photographed in the same place. Some secret spot frozen in time and space, a place that must always look a certain way despite the laws of nature and physics. A place that manifests the claustrophobic trap of conventional femininity."

MICHELLE GOOD finds her roots with the powerfully creative people of the Battle River Cree in Saskatchewan. She was raised in small-town BC and Vancouver and has traveled extensively. She presently lives in Kamloops, BC, her house perched high above the confluence of the North and South Thompson Rivers, a peaceful, inspiring place. She earned her LLB and MFA at UBC. Her poems appear in *The Puritan*, *Gathering Strength Vol VII*, and *West 49th*.

Good writes, "Rising from my grief at the death of my son, my only child, 'Defying Gravity' is an expression of incomprehensible loss and unlikely hope of renewal. The title is a double-entendre meant to convey the weightless, careless joy of summer rivers, both tangible and symbolic, juxtaposed against the drowning sensation of grief. It expresses my wistful desire to be the water of life again; to be the river that might deliver him back to me and me back to halcyon days. The poem started, less than two years after Jay died, as a long rambling wail; a grief-stricken keen; a modern-day grieving ritual, my heart excised and splattered on the page. I had the very good fortune of being able to workshop the poem with a wonderful group which, when everyone was finished crying, gave me solid perspectives on its strength as a poem. I took their notes and my own, sat in the sun, communed with that Boy of mine and 'River' became 'Defying Gravity.' I wanted this poem to be like a mantra—a way of going back using the sounds, sights and smells of rivers in their natural places to create a tangible connection to the best of times before time stopped. The title was divinely inspired. I didn't think if it. It just arrived. I feel Jay's hand in this poem, reaching to console and to remind that there is meaning and beauty in even the darkest times."

LAURIE D. GRAHAM hails from Sherwood Park, Alberta, and now lives in the Kitchener-Waterloo area. She has published two books of poetry: *Settler*

Education (McClelland & Stewart, 2016) and *Rove* (Hagios Press, 2013). Her work has won or was shortlisted for the Thomas Morton Memorial Prize, the CBC Poetry Prize, *Arc's* Poem of the Year contest, and the Gerald Lampert Memorial Award. She is the publisher of *Brick* magazine.

Graham writes, "Twice a week a train called The Canadian leaves Toronto's Union Station and travels over the Great Lakes and west to Vancouver. This train is assigned the number One, which gives you an idea of the historical significance of that route to this nation. When the train returns east they give it the number Two. Until recently, you could get yourself as far as Edmonton, with access to a bed and a shower and three square meals a day, for under four hundred bucks. It takes three days to get there. For all the plush treatment—the cloth napkins, the good soap, the champagne they pop when the train pulls out of Union Station—this is a fraught route, and that's what 'Number One Canadian' is about. Treaties were proffered and reserves were established across the prairies in part because of that train. The last moments of war on this continent took place in part because of that train—Gabriel Dumont and Louis Riel, those Métis heroes, standing up to the government's deafness and the impending loss of their land. Canada at this time was in a period of recession, so in the face of significant objection John A. Macdonald hung all the country's hopes on shipping goods manufactured in southern Ontario across the country via train. Over a century later, one Stephen Harper tried pinning the country's whole fortunes on the oilpatch, and lo and behold, it didn't work then either."

JANE EATON HAMILTON is the author of nine books of short fiction and poetry, including the 2016 novel *Weekend*. Her books have been shortlisted for the MIND Book Award, the BC Book Prize, the VanCity Award, the Pat Lowther Award and the Ferro-Grumley Award. Her memoir was one of the UK Guardian's Best Books of the Year and a Sunday Times bestseller. She is the two-time winner of Canada's CBC Literary Award for fiction (2003/2014). Her work has appeared in publications such as *Salon, En Route, Macleans*, and the *NY Times*. She lives in Vancouver.

Eaton writes, "I wrote 'Wish You Were Here' in Paris. I was living in an apartment in the 16th and had found myself the next thing to a shut-in. I made what I could of it. Every day I painted, acrylics on paper (for portability), spending no longer than an hour on each, and I taped these to the walls so that I had, by the end, a sort of art gallery of my own, pieces brightly dancing from ceiling to floor. Every day I wrote a piece of sudden fiction and a poem. I loved the swift-shooting subways, but they were hard. I could manage to maneuver the tube, but to leave the station, with the stairs, left me gasping, and there I would be, marooned by my body above the dog shit, in the midst of a Paris street scene. I'd lean myself against a lamp pole trying to still shortness of breath and angina, and a lemon would roll by. It was a Paris I would have missed with a partner or with an able body. 'Wish You Were Here' was a kind of wistful cry to my ex-life where I'd had some assistance for my disabilities, warring with a fierce 'I can manage just fine without you.' Except the truth was harder than the poem: in reality, I often wouldn't get where I was trying to go; instead, in defeat, I'd just retrace my steps."

STEVEN HEIGHTON lives in Kingston. His poetry has appeared in *London Review of Books*, *Poetry*, *TLR*, *Agni*, *The Walrus*, and recent editions of both *Best Canadian Poetry* and *Best American Poetry*. His first collection, *Stalin's Carnival*, won the 1990 Gerald Lampert Award and was recently reissued in a revised edition by Palimpsest Press. His other collections include the Governor-General's Award finalist *The Ecstasy of Skeptics*; *The Address Book*; and a new collection, *The Waking Comes Late*, which has just appeared with Anansi.

Of "In Order to Burn," Heighton writes, "I scribbled down a first draft of this poem several years ago on a scrap of paper I must have torn out of some cheap paperback. To judge by the handwriting—even messier than usual—I probably wrote the thing in the middle of the night, probably on waking after a dream. More and more often, this is how poems come to me if they come. For some years, I've had to focus on writing fiction during the days, reluctantly shunting poetry into the margins of my creative life. Apparently the poetry-writing part of my brain has compensated by working the graveyard shift: once or twice a month it hauls me awake to deliver images, phrases, metaphors, and sometimes whole (short) poems. The better ones have a sort of oneiric freshness and authenticity. Others that seem good as I scrawl them down by flashlight look like nonsense in the morning. At any rate, the challenge—if my nightmind presents me with something unfinished, as it usually does—is trying to extend and complete the poem using my very differently-wired daytime brain. But it's a challenge I relish. Through a number of drafts I was calling the poem 'Fragment of a fragment,' but eventually, as the thing became less and less fragmentary, I chose another title—a vaguely remembered phrase from a book I read years ago and can't find a trace of now. The author was Italian, I think. The book concerned romantic/erotic love and I was struck by the suggestion that the 'purpose' of such love is not so much soul-bonding and pairing as it is the provision, to each partner, of a transcendent intensity, aliveness, and awakeness: 'Tristan and Iseult require each other in order to burn.' Something like that. If anyone out there can help me nail the citation, I'd be grateful."

JASON HEROUX lives in Kingston and published *Hard Work Cheering Up Sad Machines* in the spring of 2016 with Mansfield Press. He is the author of *Memoirs of an Alias* (2004), *Emergency Hallelujah* (2008), *Good Evening, Central Laundromat* (2010), *Natural Capital* (2012) and *We Wish You a Happy Killday* (2014). His work has appeared in magazines and journals in Canada, the U.S., Belgium, France, and Italy and has been translated into French, Italian, and Arabic.

Heroux writes, "I finished reading Alfred Starr Hamilton's posthumous collection *A Dark Dreambox of Another Kind* (The Song Cave, 2013) and was struck by his ability to blend child-like wonder with adult complexities. I tried to write 'Allowance' in that same spirit. The poem started off as a stand-alone piece but eventually became part of a sequence titled The Vending Machine of Earthly Delights. I play with the title 'Allowance' as meaning both the allowance our parents give use as children, as well as the allowance to do something we're not usually permitted to do. The poem asks: how much of what we do is done because it's expected of us? Not just as children living under our parents' roof, but as citizens living under society's roof, and ultimately as organisms living under the roof of an eco-system. How do we spend the life we're allowed to live? One of the things I like most about the poem is the speaker's neutral tone, as if he's just describing the facts of life. You take the good. You take the bad. You take them both and then eventually give everything back."

GERALD HILL, the poet laureate of Saskatchewan, lives and writes in Regina. In 2015 he published his ninth poetry collection (*Hillsdale Book*, NeWest Press) and *A Round for Fifty Years: A History of Regina's Globe Theatre* (Coteau).

Of "Why We Don't Know," Hill writes, "I don't know. I don't remember. Dated January 28, 2014, the poem came from my second day in Lisbon, when I was feeling the strangeness of the new place, that strangeness we travel for, getting out of what we know, into new knowing. Of course, the process of knowing is itself an unknown dynamic. Images come, and sensations, and new versions of familiar acts like getting on a bus, banking, shopping for groceries and wine. We note these things haphazardly. We walk about more or less dazed/amazed by the splash of it all. In this poem, two of Lisbon's more obvious delights appear. One is the tram, the streetcar—a charming old shack on wheels, popular with tourists for that reason—which on certain routes runs as it has for a century or more. The old tram, electric, will rumble forward unless braked by the operator with a counter-clockwise crank of his/her horizontal wheel. To release into motion, crank it the other way. You could trot alongside as quickly as the old tram squeals and creaks its way. The second prominent Lisbon element in the poem is the historic plaza of the waterfront district rebuilt in a grid system—thought to be the height of urban sophistication at the time—after the earthquake in 1755 that destroyed the old city centre below the castle. The poem ends in imminence. It won't be another earthquake, we hope. Maybe just the next tram arriving."

AMBER HOMENIUK is kept by a small flock of hens in rural southwestern Ontario. Her writing appears in *The Malahat Review, The Fiddlehead, Numéro Cinq*, and *Windsor Review*'s tribute to Alice Munro. Amber's first chapbook is *Product of Eden: Field of Mice* (Norfolk Arts Centre, 2013). In 2015 she was shortlisted for the Montreal International Poetry Prize, and won Readers' Choice for *Arc*'s Poem of the Year with "by the time he hit the floor." butaneanvil.blogspot.ca

Homeniuk writes, "Recall and documentation of life-story conversations, with close attention to a person's use of language and symbolism, are habitual to my work as a psychotherapist. I feel likewise entrusted when designated by family to eulogize, act as M.C., and deliver merciless birthday roasts. I absorbed the essential matter of 'by the time he hit the floor' over many faceted re-tellings through the years, during gruelling and painstaking farm chores, car trips, time served in medical waiting rooms, meandering phone calls. In 2014 a swarm of honeybees graced my yard, the events of 1967 coalesced as poem. There's a particular gesture accompanying 'all that nice pink'—I wanted, for the reader, a sensation of blinking awake in the passenger seat enwrapped by a familiar voice. My earliest catalyst for connecting with poetry of home was John B. Lee's *Hired Hands* (Brick Books, 1986), a feat considering how grimly I bore my farming childhood. Other influences seaming this poem are Ivan

Coyote's storytelling and their teachings on memoir-writing, and a Douglas Glover lecture on novel structure, specifically, his thoughts on braiding imagery exemplified by Margaret Atwood's *Cat's Eye* (McClelland & Stewart, 1988). Thus, an assemblage of true facts laid out in my dad's beautiful phrasing: a death and a living in tobacco, that can of worms, all of the sweetness and sting and disintegration of courting through seasons of tragic loss, microcosm of devastation in uneaten dessert, and even good old St. Bernard of Clairvaux—patron saint of bees, and beekeepers."

MAUREEN HYNES's first book, *Rough Skin*, won the League of Canadian Poets' Gerald Lampert Award, and in 2016, her fourth, *The Poison Colour*, was nominated for both the League's Pat Lowther and Raymond Souster awards. Her poetry has been collected in over 20 anthologies, twice longlisted for the CBC Canada Reads contest, and was included in *Best Canadian Poetry in English 2010*. Maureen is poetry editor for *Our Times* magazine. www.maureenhynes.com.

Hynes writes, "'Wing On' imagines a Toronto memorial for the poet James Schuyler, who was, from the 1950s into the 70s, a key member of the New York School, along with Frank O'Hara and John Ashbery, Bernadette Mayer and Alice Notley and many others. He was a gay poet, and his explicitly gay *The Morning of the Poem* won a Pulitzer Prize in 1980. I'd studied Schuyler's work in a course offered by the poet, Hoa Nguyen, and admired his attentiveness to the details of daily life, the seemingly offhand breeziness of his style grounded in a deep knowledge of art and literature. From him, I learned a looser style of poetics. Schuyler died in 1991. I placed Schuyler's memorial service in the beautifully named 'Wing On' Chinese funeral home ('Wing On' meaning 'eternal peace' in Cantonese) that no longer exists but used to be located on Toronto's Spadina Avenue. It has always remained in my mind as a place combining grief and felicity. Some of the details in the poem are taken from Schuyler's life—the boating, the love of flowers, the financial troubles, for example. Others are taken from my own life, such as a visit to the Père Lachaise cemetery in Paris where Oscar Wilde is buried, or the sighting of teenagers outside a high school celebrating 'Pink T-Shirt Day'—small gestures pointing towards queerness. 'Wing On' is mostly a poem of appreciation for another poet. And I thank John Barton for the delightful editing exchange we had after the poem was accepted for *The Malahat*."

SALLY ITO is a poet and translator of poetry who lives in Winnipeg, Manitoba. She has published three books of poetry, her most recent being *Alert to Glory*, published in 2011 by Turnstone Press. With co-translator Michiko Tsuboi, Ito's translations of Japanese children's poetry by Misuzu Kaneko will be published in a picture book, *Are you an Echo? The Lost Poetry of Misuzu Kaneko* by Chin Music Press in the fall of 2016.

Of "Idle," Ito writes, "I wrote this poem thinking about 'idleness' as a state-of-mind experienced in the church pew. To sit through a weekly church service is a spiritual discipline that while seemingly boring actually serves to bring one in alignment with oneself, one's God, and one's faith community. 'Idleness' is also that gestational state often associated with creativity where the artist appears to be doing nothing, but is actually 'awaiting' inspiration, as it were. Sometimes we need to be 'put' into that space before anything arises from out of it."

AMANDA JERNIGAN grew up in rural Ontario. She lived for many years on the east coast of Canada, before returning to Ontario (Hamilton), in 2010. She is the author of two books of poems, *Groundwork* (2011) and *All the Daylight Hours* (2013), and of the monograph *Living in the Orchard: The Poetry of Peter Sanger* (2014). Her work has appeared in magazines in Canada, the U.S., and the U.K.

Of "Engraving," Jernigan writes, "The titular engraving is, amongst other things, Dürer's famous *Ritter, Tod und Teufel* (Knight, Death, and the Devil): in particular a specific, late-off-the-block copy of this work that hung on the wall in my grandparents' house, exiled to a spot beneath the basement stairs— where, as my mother tells me, it used to scare her rigid, when she was a child. I returned to this print, myself, after my second son was born, following a week spent with him in hospital as he recovered from an unexpected, early-weeks illness. And I thought: obviously (such is the sleep-deprived insight of new motherhood), Dürer's knight is a woman, and her breastplate conceals no mead-paunch but a child. 'This is the way the ladies ride' is from the nursery rhyme, and an echo of Eliot in its triple iteration. I'm something of a collagist, when I'm writing poetry. Poems happen when multiple bits of read and lived experience line up in superimposition, like stacked transparencies: the Dürer engraving, the fairytale cliché of the woman incognito in knight's armour, the experience of trying to nurse (literally and figuratively) a baby through its first weeks of life, the nursery rhyme, the Eliot. There's a Borges poem in there, too.

Though I always hope a poem will turn out to be more than the sum of its allusions. The title, 'Engraving,' with its etymological gravity, came last, and out of nowhere: obvious, but a gift."

KATE KENNEDY is from Lillooet, BC. After many years in the Maritimes, she now lives in Victoria. Her poetry has been published in numerous journals, including *The Fiddlehead*, *The Malahat Review*, *The Antigonish Review*, *Ryga*, and *PRISM*, and was selected for 2013's *Best Canadian Poetry in English*. (Thoughts on reading, writing and editing: katekennedyeditor.com and @ katekeditor)

Of "Late Changes in the Homescape," Kennedy writes, "I wrote this poem after spending most of a summer at my family's place outside Lillooet, BC. Since leaving for university, I had visited many times for shorter stints, but this stretch was long enough for me to hang around in some of the odd corners of the property I'd mostly ignored since I was a kid. That summer our older dog was on a steady decline and continually finding himself in awkward situations. At the same time our barn was, structurally, well on its way to becoming a death trap and so was slated to be torn down. But throughout the summer the dog remained in what seemed like impossibly good spirits even on 40-degree days, mostly oblivious to his age and to the discussions going on around him about his heart and his quality of life. And of course the barn had no idea what was in store for it. I had two poems in mind at first, but after I started writing, the dog and the barn began to seem not so dissimilar, in their indifference and hopefulness. My sense of doom didn't factor into their days at all and that became more interesting to me than the pair of obituaries I'd first sat down to write."

M. TRAVIS LANE lives in Fredericton, New Brunswick, and has published fifteen books of poetry, the most recent: *The Crisp Day Closing on my Hand*, Wilfred Laurier University Press, 2007, *The Book of Widows*, Frog Hollow Press, 2010, *The All-Nighter's Radio*, from Guernica in 2010, *Ash Steps*, from Cormorant in 2012, and *Crossover*, also from Cormorant in 2015. Also appearing in 2015: *The Essential M. Travis Lane*, selected poems, from Porcupine's Quill, *How Thought Feels, the Poetry of M. Travis Lane*, Frog Hollow Press, and expected in 2016, *The Complete Long Poems of M. Travis Lane*, from Goose Lane Editions, and *Heart on Fist: selected prose of M. Travis Lane*, Palimpsest Press.

Of "A Little Advice From the Matriarch," Lane writes, "We receive a great deal of advice from our parents and grandparents —but the advice we remember best is the advice they inherited from their parents and grandparents, and pass on in 'sayings.' A 'saying' might be advice; it might be simply an observation. A 'saying' is not a koan, an apparent paradox for meditation, nor a gatha, a verse to help us live more mindfully. Nor are they invariably useful, gratefully received, or graciously intended. 'A Little Advice From the Matriarch' is that sort of thing, i.e.: 'My momma done tole me.'"

JEFF LATOSIK lives in Toronto. His work has appeared in various Canadian magazines and journals. Work from his second collection, *Safely Home Pacific Western*, was nominated for a national magazine award and included in the *Best Canadian Poetry Series* for 2015. He is also the author of the poetry collection *Tiny, Frantic, Stronger* (2010).

Latosik writes, "Thank you for plucking 'The Internet' out of the void. It was cut from my second collection *Safely Home Pacific Western* and probably won't be included in a subsequent book. So it remains in this interesting twice-published, of that book, perhaps the key poem of my second book, but not in that book—in this one. State. I did first hear about the Internet in my job at Burger King when I was about 14 years old. It's just like any other sort of weird thing you remember and that stays with you over time. Of course, the future was something completely different then to my imagination: it was about material innovation; it was about rockets and flying cars and crystalline sound. That was part of an old world that I interpreted as new, and I guess what strikes me as strange about the memory was just how small and almost unnoticeable actual history was, passing by me. The new was almost unnoticeable. Almost. Where is the Internet? Where is this poem? In two places, and not the place its author intended it to be. It's the key poem of a book it wasn't published in. Seems a fitting ending point for an Internet poem."

EVELYN LAU is a Vancouver writer who has published eleven books, including six volumes of poetry. Her work has received the Milton Acorn Award, the Pat Lowther Award, a National Magazine Award, and a Governor-General's nomination; she served as 2011-2014 Poet Laureate for the City of Vancouver. Her next collection, *Tumour*, is forthcoming from Oolichan Books.

Of "Mid-Autumn Festival," Lau writes, "Everything tastes better when it's shared, Oprah once said. But what about private gluttony, the shame that attaches to quantities of food consumed in secret? For many women food is a complicated enough pleasure; when you toss in some cultural baggage, it becomes even more fraught. In this poem the moon cakes symbolize everything I spurned (family, obligation, tradition), yet in some way still hungered for. Does food represent love given, love withheld? For years I ricocheted between bingeing and self-denial, and the poem attempts to capture both the lure and the repulsion, the gorging and its aftermath. In the last two stanzas, the story of the monks comes from a New Yorker article about the rigorous training monks endure in traditional Japanese temples; this anecdote echoes the theme of starvation versus satiation in the rest of the poem."

RANDY LUNDY is a member of the Barren Lands (Cree) First Nation. Born in northern Manitoba, he has lived most of his life in Saskatchewan. He has published two previous books, *Under the Night Sun* and *Gift of the Hawk*. 2016 will see the publication of a third book of poems, *Blackbird Song*. Randy also writes short stories and is currently working on a manuscript for publication. Randy teaches Indigenous literatures and creative writing in the English Department at Campion College, University of Regina.

Lundy writes, "'An Ecology of Being and Non-Being' began in the way that most of my poems begin—just for fun. Just to see what power words might display. Words are animals; they are dogs, or horses, or raptors. Actually they are all of these things. Much of my recent writing tries to make some peace between Buddhism and my Indigenous identity. Being and non-being are like Yin and Yang—you can't have one without the other. Each is dependant upon the other. Cree playwright Tomson Highway talks about losing his brother Rene to AIDS and goes on to speak about how he is not sad about the loss because his brother is still with him all the time. I think Highway is talking about a relationship between life and death that mirrors the relationship between being and non-being. Can't have one without the other, and really the two are never separate. Hence, 'there is no need to grieve.' Just make offerings and trust."

SNEHA MADHAVAN-REESE was born in Detroit and now lives with her family in Ottawa. Her debut poetry collection is *Observing the Moon* (Hagios Press, 2015). Her poem "Rosa Parks" won *Arc Poetry Magazine*'s 2015 Diana Brebner Prize.

Of "Rosa Parks," Madhavan-Reese writes, "On November 1, 2005, civil rights activist Rosa Parks lay in repose at the Charles H. Wright Museum of African-American History in Detroit. I was privileged to witness that historic event. The day percolated in my mind for many years, until it became this poem."

LEE MARACLE is the author of a number of critically acclaimed literary works and is the co-editor of a number of anthologies including the award-winning publication, *My Home As I Remember*. Ms. Maracle is a member of the Sto: Loh nation. In 2009, Maracle received an Honorary Doctor of Letters from St. Thomas University. Maracle recently received the Queen's Diamond Jubilee Medal and the premier's award for excellence in the arts. Her latest works are: *Celia's Song* (novel), *Memory Serves and other Words* (creative non-fiction) and *Talking to the Diaspora*.

In a *nineteenquestions.com* interview about her writing Maracle says, "I think every writer makes a sacrifice. You have a deadline to meet and you meet it. You give up things for art and I gave up a couple of husbands for it... Whatever needs to be done for the art you do it."

STEPHEN MAUDE lives in Toronto. His writing has appeared in *The Antigonish Review*, *Echolocation*, *FreeFall*, *The New Quarterly*, *Qwerty*, and on *Feathertale.com*.

Maude writes, "Sometimes a poem originates as a patchwork of thoughts, memories, and imaginings. 'I Run With You Still' began this way, as a threading together of my passion for running with recollections of a trip to Vancouver Island and many summers spent at a family cottage near Lake Simcoe. From there it evolved into a narrative about friendship and memory and loss. It explores a paradox: we think of ourselves as insignificant in the context of a contingent universe and yet we value beyond measure the happy accidents of our lives and loves and friendships. It also notes, with some regret, that the love between friends, though profound, often remains unspoken."

CASSIDY MCFADZEAN lives in Regina. She is the author of *Hacker Packer* (McClelland & Stewart 2015), shortlisted for two Saskatchewan Book Awards and the Gerald Lampert Memorial Award. Her work has appeared in magazines across Canada including *The Malahat Review*, *Grain*, and *The Fiddlehead*, and has been a finalist for the CBC Poetry Prize and the *Walrus*

Poetry Prize. Cassidy graduated from the Iowa Writers' Workshop in 2015 and now teaches as a sessional lecturer.

Of "Nymph," McFadzean writes, "I read Charles Martin's translation of *Metamorphoses* in the summer of 2014 and was enthralled with Ovid's descriptions of figures shifting between the human and animal worlds. I've found Nietzsche's conception of the Apollonian and the Dionysian useful in articulating the control and chaos many of my poems seem to explore, and I've always been fascinated by Greek mythology and creatures such as satyrs that veer between these worlds. This was the summer I found myself caught between worlds; I was in between the two years of my MFA degree, and camping with my parents in Revelstoke, BC days before leaving for Iceland—a country rich with its own mythology. One day, I went out in the forest behind their campsite with my younger brother. The forest in Revelstoke is filled with moss and ferns, and my brother and I decided to go off the path, venturing up the steep incline of the mountain. Many of the events in the poem happened more or less as I describe them; I fell in a brook, scratched my legs, and seemed to stumble from tree to tree as if lost or drunk—trapped in an Ovidian myth. When I grabbed a tree to balance myself and its thin branch slipped itself under my wedding ring, it was hard not to feel myself transformed and 'wedded' to the forest. I thought of Ovid's description of the nymph Daphne escaping Apollo by transforming into a laurel tree, and I knew I'd found my title."

DAVID MCGIMPSEY lives in Montreal and is the author of six collections of poetry including *Asbestos Heights* (Coach House Books), which was named by CBC Books as one of the "Best Books of 2015" and was the winner of 2015's A.M. Klein Award for Poetry. His previous volume, *Li'l Bastard*, was nominated for the Governor General's Award. David McGimpsey is also the author of the short fiction collection *Certifiable* and the award-winning critical study *Imagining Baseball: America's Pastime and Popular Culture*. Named by the CBC as one of the "Top Ten English language poets in Canada" his work was also the subject of the book of essays *Population Me: Essays on David McGimpsey*. David is the Montreal fiction editor to *Joyland* magazine and is a food and travel writer who regularly contributes to *EnRoute* magazine. A PhD in American Literature, David McGimpsey teaches in the English Department of Concordia University.

Of "When Sylvia Plath said 'People or stars regard me sadly' I think she mostly meant 'people,'" McGimpsey writes, "The poem is a satire of creative writing pedagogy and the kind of writing advice that feels motivated by class-conscious pop psychology. The sonnet-like structure seeks to hold its rhetoric in a familiar place while knowing that writers of poetry have zero responsibility and are not asked much beyond that they possess some kind of 'elevated' taste. The laugh is plotted as a recognition-laugh about how poetry is organized around social capital (the 'people' of Plath's quote) and not consumer capital."

STEVE MCORMOND is a native of Prince Edward Island and has made his home in Toronto since 1997. His most recent book of poetry is *The Good News about Armageddon* (Brick Books 2010). His previous collection *Primer on the Hereafter* (Wolsak and Wynn 2006) was awarded the Atlantic Poetry Prize. His poems have appeared in *Arc, Cordite* (Australia), *CV2, Lemon Hound, Malahat Review* and *Poetry Daily*. www.stevemcormond.com

Of "All-Inclusive," McOrmond writes, "The figures and setting are archetypal, the dance at once contemporary and timeless: Is there a more universally human pattern than the figure eight? In stumbling upon this scene and observing the distances—geographic, cultural, socio-economic—between the two figures and the longing for connection that brings them into guarded proximity, the poem considers the bonds that can't be kept at bay. It unsettles the notion that we can ever 'get away from it all' in our current hyper-connected and technology-dominated age. Set against a backdrop of deep time and deep space, an all-encompassing darkness and silence (a different species of noise) that is always on the verge of consuming us, the figures' anxious, wordless dance reminds us of our tininess, but also our tenacity and courage in pushing back against the infinite. Rereading the poem now, I'm reminded of a line from James Schuyler's poem 'The Smallest': 'It is infinite and therefore the smallest thing.'"

A.F. MORITZ lives in Toronto; his most recent book is *Sequence* (House of Anansi Press, 2015). *The New Measures* (2012) received the Raymond Souster Award of the League of Canadian Poets and was a Governor General's Award finalist, and his 2008 collection, *The Sentinel*, was awarded the Griffin Poetry Prize and the Bess Hokin Prize of *Poetry* magazine. In 2015 Princeton University Press republished his 1986 book *The Tradition*.

Of "The Clock," Moritz writes, "Maybe this poem is generated not only by its own subject but by Poe, his keen prophetic grasp of so much of modernity under the image and experience of hyperaesthesia. Maybe a painfully fascinated awareness of the commonest things, those most in the background, things scarcely seen or heard—things even unseen and unheard because we only fear or imagine they may exist—until, suddenly, they emerge as thunder, preoccupation, obsession, insomnia, paranoia...maybe this has always been part of humans. But it's certainly part of today. We fear to hear, to sense, the heart's beating and the pulse, and this fear is exaggerated by—does it perhaps originate from?—the ticking of the clock. The blood: the clock—that similar, parallel rhythm we've created to emphasize the fewness of the shortness of our breaths and days. To assert, even if it does not really exist, an external mechanical dimension to reality, not even 'opposed to' what we feel as ourselves, but simply unrelated to it in any way. Irrelevant, and entirely encompassing, overwhelming, dominant. The premature burial. The original monstrous and invulnerable alien. There is the fact that even rest is a torrent. But, then, the poem's end, as it contends to be what encloses and lies at the centre, glimpses that the torrent is rest. The storm, the disaster, the being-dragged-along, inheres in the subsequent, and the former, rest. Poe."

HOA NYUGEN, born in the Mekong Delta and raised in the Washington, D.C. area, currently makes her home in Toronto. She is the author of *As Long As Trees Last*, *Red Juice: Poems 1998-2008*, and *Violet Energy Ingots* (all from Wave Books). Nguyen teaches at Ryerson University, for Miami University's low residency MFA program, in the Milton Avery School for Fine Arts at Bard College, and in her own long-running, private poetics workshop.

Of "From the Autobiography of Malcolm X," Nguyen writes, "In the summer of 2015, in preparation for teaching *S.O.S.*, a volume of selected poems by the late Amiri Baraka, I studied a constellation of works and writings: scholarly essays, articles, lectures, interviews, music, plays, and poems. I read Baraka's groundbreaking work 'Blues People,' a cultural study of the history of black music in the Americas, a book written in 1963, the year of the March on Washington, the assassination of Medgar Evers, and the bombing of a Birmingham church that killed four black girls. As part of my study of US human rights activism history, I also read *The Autobiography of Malcolm X* as told to Alex Haley. When I read the latter, I hadn't expected how it would affect me. The narratives from the outset were horrific: Malcolm X's family terrorized by the white people in their community, his father murdered by the same people, his mother driven mentally ill from the subsequent stress and anguish (including grim poverty), his siblings taken from the home and split up. It was gripping to read how he rose out of that circumstance to become a leader in the struggle for human rights against the backdrop of entrenched systemic racism and anti-blackness. It was around this time that I was challenged to write a 'found' poem: to take compelling language from a prose source and arrange into verse. This poem represents a sentence from toward the end of this book that hit me, squarely, with its sure truth."

ELISE PARTRIDGE was a finalist for the BC Book Prize and the Gerald Lampert Award and won the Canadian Authors Association Poetry Award. Partridge's work has been anthologized in Canada, the U.S., Ireland, and the U.K. The poem "The Exile's Home Gallery" appeared in Partridge's third and final collection, *The Exiles' Gallery* (House of Anansi, 2015). She died in February of 2015.

MATT RADER was born and raised on Vancouver Island. He lives in the Okanagan Valley in the BC interior where he teaches Creative Writing at the University of British Columbia Okanagan. His most recent book of poems is *Desecrations* (McClelland & Stewart 2016).

Of "Mavis Gallant," Rader writes, "In 2013 and 2014 I stayed in the Maldron Hotel in Cork, Ireland, just below the Shandon Bell tower with its four clock faces that each tell a different time. A modest hotel chain, the Cork iteration of Maldron hotels exists in a former hospital for the poor. During my second visit I spent some time in the Cork City archives reading about the building's history. Meanwhile, my friend had her first baby. I read a lot of books written by women. I wrote poems for my friends. Who knows how it all comes together, but as it did I heard first the voice of John Berryman ventriloquized, then Maggie Nelson chipping in her pithy observation about boredom and solitude. Then there was a poem. The clock tower is known locally as the 'Four-faced Liar.'"

RACHEL ROSE has won poetry, fiction, and non-fiction awards, including a 2016 Pushcart Prize. Recently a fellow at The University of Iowa's International Writing Program, she is the Poet Laureate of Vancouver. A chapbook, *Thirteen Ways of Looking at CanLit*, (BookThug) and a poetry collection, *Marry & Burn* (Harbour) were published in 2015. Her non-fiction book, *Gone to the Dogs:*

Riding Shotgun with K9 Cops, is forthcoming from St. Martin's Press/Thomas Dunne Books (rachelsprose.weebly.com/).

Rose writes, "I will share two notes that may perhaps be of interest to readers of this poem. When I first moved into the house that appears in the poem, 'Good Measure,' for three days running a grandmother appeared in my yard, wringing her hands at the divorce of her daughter that had led to the sale of the house to us. Inside the house, as I repainted, I found the marks of those first children in the doorframe, marked at different ages, different heights, stubborn marks deep in the wood that resisted being painted over. What you can't see when reading 'Good Measure' in this anthology is that it follows a crown of sonnets in my collection *Marry & Burn*. The sonnet series riffs on a dog's life and death, and charts a marriage. The dog is cremated and buried in the yard. The sonnet ends with this line: 'Now we can never leave this house.'" 'Good Measure' takes up where 'Corona' leaves off—the house has been left, the vows broken, the relationship cracked open. The unthinkable has become the present act. The speaker's use of repetition is a lament for all that has been lost—eulogy for a family home."

ARMAND GARNET RUFFO is a scholar and poet of Ojibway heritage. He is recognized as one of the earliest contributors to contemporary Indigenous literature and Indigenous literary criticism in Canada. His work includes *The Thunderbird Poems*, (Harbour Publishing, 2015), which was nominated for the Raymond Souster Award, and a creative biography, *Norval Morrisseau: Man Changing Into Thunderbird* (Douglas & McIntyre, 2014), nominated for the Governor General's Literary Award. Ruffo teaches at Queen's University in Kingston.

Ruffo writes, "So much has been forgotten about the land. Glance at a road sign, the name of a lake, a marsh, a hill, a community, written in one of the many languages indigenous to this continent. What does it tell you? Probably not much. If you understand the language (at least have an inkling) however the land opens up to you, and you become connected in a way you never though possible. It is both an intellectual and physical connection that, as I say in the poem, plunges into you like a stake. This is the process the Ojibway artist Norval Morrisseau went through while apprenticing with his grandfather Potan Nanakonagos, and it is something I strive to 'translate' for the reader throughout *The Thunderbird Poems*, a suite of ekphrastic poems inspired by the artist's work. My goal is to bring you into the experience of connecting to Anishinaabe epistemology and mythology. From a 21st Century perspective, the arrogance of settler-society to try to erase Indigenous language(s) from the very land it arose from is mind-boggling, and the tragic consequences are well documented, not only for Indigenous peoples but for all Canadians, especially when so many people now realize that nature is a living breathing life-force that inhabits us as much as we inhabit it. This is a central element of the book, and 'Sacred Beaver, 1969' exemplifies this idea by attempting to get inside Norval's painting while considering it in terms of the artist's own spiritual growth."

DOUGLAS BURNET SMITH was born in Winnipeg, but has resided in Antigonish, Nova Scotia for the past three decades. He is the author of sixteen books of poems. His work has been nominated for the Governor General's Award for poetry and the Atlantic Poetry Prize. In 2015, he was a finalist in the National Magazine Awards for poetry. *Learning To Count* (Frontenac House) was selected as one of the *Globe and Mail*'s Best 100 books of 2010. Smith has served as president of The League of Canadian Poets and as Chair of The Public Lending Right Commission of Canada. He teaches at St. Francis Xavier University and occasionally at The American University of Paris.

Smith writes, "'Mosquitoes, Scissors, Stars' is part of a section of poems from a work-in-progress about growing up in Winnipeg in the 1950s, a generally hideous time of compulsory homogeneity which demanded macho behaviour from males of all ages, but especially from impressionable young boys. (It's now 2016. Some things do never change). At the time, Winnipeg experienced the highest incidence of polio cases per capita in North America. The disease crippled people that I knew, from my very own neighbourhood. My friends and I tacitly decided the best way to fend off this 'plague' would be to render oneself immune by becoming as tough as possible, and so we devised the ritual of allowing Winnipeg's legendary, ferocious mosquitoes to take our blood as we stood, almost entirely naked, during hot summer evenings on our irrigated front lawns in Silver Heights. The boy who outlasted all the others would win. But even if you didn't win, you would be building resistance, we intuited, to polio. So no one really lost. Or lost face, at least. In the mild agony of this perverse endurance contest, I think we did achieve a kind of exstasis, standing outside ourselves, gazing back at ourselves as miniature heroes. So the mosquito scene described in the poem actually happened; at least I think it did. Peering back so many decades, it's hard to say for sure. As for the rest of the poem, involving my mother, I can't, or won't, say it did or didn't happen: it's wonderfully strange how the imagination can invent, or at least unintentionally elaborate upon, 'memory.'"

KILBY SMITH-MCGREGOR lives in Toronto, where she spent her early professional life making theatre. Writing across genres, she has contributed to *Conjunctions*, *The Kenyon Review*, *Brick*, *Descant*, *The Malahat Review*, *The Puritan* and *Best Canadian Essays*. Kilby won the Writers' Trust of Canada's 2010 RBC Bronwen Wallace Award and holds an MFA from the University of Guelph. Her debut poetry collection, *Kids in Triage*, was recently published by Wolsak & Wynn.

Of "Wake Up Remembering Oranges," Smith-McGregor writes, "Returning to university in my mid-twenties to complete my BA, I granted myself permission to study writing for the first time. I was counting on formal education to offer up classical models and frameworks to deconstruct, and I wasn't disappointed. This piece came out of my third year York University poetry class. The necessarily obsessive qualities of the villanelle—of which this poem is an example—provided an elegant challenge. My desire was to offset the heightened frame with contemporary vernacular and domestic content. I wanted it to feel at once incidental and inevitable in form, and act, to some degree, as an expression of shock. Villanelles can sometimes rest on an abstract declarative quality; it was important to me to create a narrative with human stakes, and a bit of a turn or complication in what the repeated language might come to signify by the end of the poem. Process-wise, the title line came first, and then I worked to carve out the world and context through trial and error, much as I might do for a short story."

KAREN SOLIE was born in Moose Jaw, grew up in rural southwest Saskatchewan, and lives in Toronto. She is the author of four collections of poems, most recently *The Road In Is Not the Same Road Out*, published in Canada and the U.S. in 2015. A volume of selected and new poems was published in the U.K. in 2013. She has taught writing for a number of universities and writing programs across Canada, and is an associate director for the Banff Centre's Writing Studio.

Solie writes, "'Forty' is set on the Isle of Mull, Scotland. The Latin name for onion, as it turns out, is *cepa*, borrowed, according to the Online Etymological Dictionary, from an unknown language. The word 'onion' derives from the Anglo-French union, Old French *oignon* 'onion' (formerly also *oingnon*), and directly from Latin *unionem* (nominative *unio*), colloquial rustic Roman for 'a kind of onion,' also 'pearl' (via notion of a string of onions), literally 'one, unity.'"

JOHN STEFFLER was born in Toronto. After living more than thirty years in Newfoundland he now divides his time between rural eastern Ontario and Montreal. His most recent book is the novel *German Mills* (Gaspereau, 2015). In 2015 Brick Books reissued his poetry collection *The Grey Islands* as part of their twenty-fifth anniversary series. His collection *Lookout* (M&S, 2010) was shortlisted for the Griffin Prize. From 2006 to 2009 he was Poet Laureate of Canada.

Of "I Haven't Looked at These in Years" Steffler writers, "The species of the speaker here is ambiguous. Looking at old family photos and slides is likely to stir up complex emotions and thoughts. We see images, often clumsy homely ones, of people and a world that have vanished into the past but which we still carry within us, people and a world that in some ways we long for and regret and yet also hate—our old selves included. There are the forces and personalities that shaped us, the rules, the fashions, the obsessions and superstitions and fears and fantasies and loves and vanities. Their traces probably now seem ordinary, arbitrary and crude. The generic drive to live and fulfill oneself can wear such different guises. Growing, becoming oneself seems to have been a struggle to emerge from some blind brutal state and become more human. But this never seems to end. Many of our characteristically human traits are hard to admire and accept."

KATE SUTHERLAND was born in Scotland, grew up in Saskatchewan, and now lives in Toronto, where she is a professor at Osgoode Hall Law School. She is the author of two collections of short stories: *Summer Reading* (winner of a Saskatchewan Book Award for Best First Book) and *All In Together Girls*. Her first book of poems, *How to Draw a Rhinoceros*, will be published by BookThug in the fall of 2016.

Sutherland writes, "I had been working on a series of rhinoceros poems for some time already when I embarked on 'Elephant v. Rhinoceros,' and was deep in the rhinoceros lore contained in centuries of natural history tomes. I was struck by the recurring assertions that I found there of enmity between elephants and rhinoceroses. Given their status as the two largest land mammals still among us, I guess it's not surprising that they would be imaginatively pitted against one another, nor that the fiercer-looking rhinoceros would be repeatedly portrayed as the villain. But the tenaciousness of the idea despite the long-term peaceful co-existence of these mostly gentle herbivores seemed perverse. I quashed my initial impulse to write in defence of the rhinoceros, and opted instead to pit the various texts I'd encountered against one another. I'm a lawyer and a law professor as well as a writer, and so perhaps naturally conceptualized a trial between the beasts with the poem ultimately taking the form of an approximation of a legal decision. The bias of the source material leaves little doubt as to the outcome. But I hope there's plenty of room between the lines for readers to arrive at their own conclusions while relishing the oddity of the historical narratives."

SYLVIA SYMONS spent most of her childhood near Prince George, BC. She now lives with her husband and sons in Vancouver where she teaches ESL at Langara College. She is currently enrolled in the Writer's Studio 2016 at Simon Fraser University. Her poem "Duffle" which appeared in *EVENT* magazine, is her first publication.

Symons writes, When I was a kid I remember listening in on adult conversation and storing the troublesome bits for later examination. I think this is pretty common. In my poem "Duffle," the child narrator rehashes an adult conversation in her head. She fixates on words as a way of distancing herself from a shameful situation. She is piecing together her first inklings of class. While I was writing this poem, I grew nostalgic for the SS Kresge's Department Store. Kresgie's in Prince George—as I knew it in the '70s- didn't sell duffle coats but it had every colour of budgie in aisle 5.

JOHN TERPSTRA's most recent book of poetry, *Brilliant Falls* (Gaspereau Press), was short-listed for the Raymond Souster Award and won the Hamilton Literary Award. His work has won the CBC Radio Literary Competition and the Bressani Prize, and also been short-listed for the Governor-General's Award. His poem, "Giants," is a Project Bookmarks plaque that stands on the top of the Niagara Escarpment overlooking downtown Hamilton, where he lives.

Of the poem "Vocation," Terpstra writes, "It's a bit embarrassing to admit that your sources of inspiration may not have been high literature or art. And it is always interesting to look back and reread an old experience through a new lens. So it is, on both counts, with this poem. Although T.S. Eliot may have been my first real, inspirational kick in the butt, the one that sent me to the typewriter to pound out my own inexplicable, footnote-worthy words and lines, the radio songs of my childhood had already set the stage. I had always understood that summer when I was ten years old to have been an illustration of my own passivity and lack of initiative. And maybe it was. But it was also an opportunity for the part of me that I did not yet know existed, the main part of me, the artistic part, to be served. It's like being made to sit in the corner in silence and discovering astral projection. Sort of. What interests me is that it was the writing of the poem itself, which led me now, half a century later, to see how that seemingly lost time long ago has all along been redeemed."

SOUVANKHAM THAMMAVONGSA is the author of three poetry books, *Small Arguments* (2003), *Found* (2007), and *Light* (2013). She won the Trillium Book Award for Poetry in 2014.

Thammavongsa writes, "It used to be expensive to take photographs. You didn't get a chance to see how your photograph would turn out before you had them printed. And you had to have them printed in order to see them. I had this photograph of a ceiling and wondered why I had taken a photo of this ceiling. Then I noticed the piece of the tree and remembered how excited I had been about having a real pine tree that Christmas. My childhood best friend, Gayatri, came over after school to look at this real tree and we thought we should take a photograph of ourselves in front of it, but instead I had aimed it at the ceiling and not at us. I didn't know we weren't in the photograph until it was developed and my parents were upset that they had to pay for this photograph of a ceiling. I have not seen Gayatri for almost twenty years and while this photograph does not have her in it, it made me think of her and of us and I saw her in a way I hadn't seen when we were children. I would not have thought so hard and so much of this photograph had we actually been in it. I thought this photograph of the ceiling captured more accurately and precisely the feeling of our friendship than one that included us. To put it another way, the failure of the photograph and the way in which it failed gave me more than one that turned out right. Once I saw that, I felt I had to write a poem about it."

NICK THRAN is the author of three collections of poems: *Mayor Snow*, *Earworm*, and *Every Inadequate Name*. He works as a poetry editor for Brick Books. Born in Prince George, British Columbia, Nick has lived and worked in various towns and cities across Canada. He has recently relocated to Fredericton, New Brunswick, and will hopefully be there for a long, long time.

Thran writes, "Sample visitors to Al and Eurithe Purdy's A-frame from September 1st 2014 to November 21st, 2014: five young Ottawa poets in a Honda Accord, two drone pilots, Eurithe Purdy, Gabe Foreman, a neighbour who pulled her canoe onto shore. Sample Purdy literature read or reread during residency: *Beyond Remembering: Collected Poems*; *We Go Far Back in Time: the Letters of Earle Birney and Al Purdy, 1947-1987*; *The Ivory Thought: Essays on Al Purdy*; *The Last Canadian Poet: An Essay on Al Purdy*. Sample animals and insects encountered within the house: mice, wasps, spiders, squirrels. Sample literature read or reread as a tonic or an alternative to Purdy literature: *White Girls* (Hilton Als), *The Empathy Exams* (Leslie Jamison), *Byssus* (Jen Hadfield), *The Beauty of the Husband* (Anne Carson). Sample work written during stay: 'Local Weirdos,' about forty percent of a book called *Mayor Snow*. Sample structure of a typical day at the A-frame: 7-11:30am, mind infant; 12:30-5pm, read and write; 5:30-7:30pm (with partner), cook meal for infant, bathe infant, put infant to bed; 8pm-10pm, read, or watch the *Lord of the Rings* trilogy. Sample dishes broken around dinnertime on account of fatigue: one porcelain serving dish, two Canadian Centennial commemorative cups (representing the provinces of Nova Scotia and British Columbia, respectively), one coffee pot."

TARA-MICHELLE ZINIUK was born in Montreal and currently lives in Toronto. She is the author of *Whatever, Iceberg* (Mansfield Press, 2016), *Somewhere To Run From* (Tightrope Books, 2009) and *Emergency Contact* (McGilligan Books, 2006). In addition to *Taddle Creek*, where this poem was originally published, her work has appeared in various print and digital publications, including *Matrix*, *PRISM*, *make/shift*, *This Magazine* and *Joyland*.

Of "By the Lachine Canal I Sat Down and..." Ziniuk writes, "My poems, this one included, are often very literal recaps of experiences where it feels impossible not to read into things. What am I doing in Montreal? What is this blue bird doing here? I was at the Rosemont overpass, feeling like I had a decade prior by the canal. Montreal is the only place I've consistently returned to throughout my life. It's impossibly timeless, for better and worse. A visceral experience in Montreal easily resurfaces others like it. Sometimes the timelessness feels like a lack of progress, whether that's about my own aging or moving through cultural moments. I was feeling that 'you can leave, but you can never really leave.' I was out of town, newly into a breakup, but with technology, and in a city where my recent ex and I both had history and emotional attachments. This relationship ending felt both very specific and very familiar in that space. The relationship itself had been quite cyclical, so it was hard to adjust to being somewhere outside of our usual loop. Then this all becomes a bit meta in that much of the relationship was spent connecting about patterns. And an acknowledged investment in serendipity, in a sense: timing and synchronicity working out. I was very against the idea that it hadn't, and hoping and looking for signs to the contrary. I can't remember if the bird was real. I wonder now if I was trying to force a resolution or alternate (literal) ending by imagining it.".

NOTABLE POEMS OF 2015 ❧

Selected by the editors (in alphabetical order by author's name)

Mark Abley — "Zoo" *Queen's Quarterly* Vol. 122.4

Najwa Ali — "Harbour" *Room* Vol. 38.1

Marie Annharte Baker — "Walk a Mile in Her Red High Heels" *Room* Vol. 38.4

Ashley-Elizabeth Best — "Living in the Wait" *Literary Review of Canada* Vol. 23.9

Tamiko Beyer — "Lean Dream" *Contemporary Verse 2* Summer 2015

Beverley Bie Brahic — "New Year" *Queen's Quarterly* Vol. 122.4

Ronna Bloom — "In the Sober Light of September" *canadianpoetries* September 1, 2015

Mary Lee Bragg — "Living in Public" *Windsor Review* Vol. 48.2

Louise Carson — "Snow Fort in Carport" *Literary Review of Canada* Vol. 23.10

Terry Ann Carter — "Untitled" *Windsor Review* Vol. 48.2

Sandra Davies — "Like Water" *The New Quarterly* Summer 2015

Michelle Marie Desmarais — "change (medicine in academe)" *Room* Vol. 38.1

Catherine Dorion (trans. Alexander Rock) — "We will not be difficult" *The Puritan* Summer 2015 supplement

Margaret Slavin Dyment — "Still Real" *Windsor Review* Vol. 48.2

Patrick Friesen — "born, going deaf" *The New Quarterly* Summer 2015

Carole Giangrande — "Spring Unsettled" *Queen's Quarterly* Vol. 122.2

Catherine Graham — "Kick the Can" *Taddle Creek* Winter 2014/2015

Philippe Haeck (trans. Scott Marentette) — excerpt from "Pour l'action" *The Puritan* Summer 2015 supplement

Richard Harrison	"Confessional Poem" *FreeFall* Vol. XXV No. 3
Stevie Howell	"Subplot" *The Malahat Review* Autumn 2015
Eve Joseph	Five Poems *The New Quarterly* Summer 2015
Jennifer Knowlan	"Crowbar" *The Antigonish Review* Winter 2015
John B. Lee	"A Person on Business from Porlock" *Windsor Review* Vol. 48.2
Alex Leslie	"Sleepers" *Contemporary Verse 2* Summer 2015
Alice Major	"11. $d = (X-x)2 + (Y-y)2 + (Z-z)2 - c(T-t)$: now" *The New Quarterly* Summer 2015
Maryann Martin	"Blue Elephant" *The New Quarterly* Summer 2015
Jeredith Merrin	"The Great Grey Owl" *The Fiddlehead*
Roger Nash	"Mystery Phone Call" *Windsor Review* Vol. 48.2
Alexandra Oliver	"Kelvinbridge, Glasgow, 2 pm" *Partisan* September 23, 2015
Eric Ormsby	"Apology for Grandmothers" *Partisan* May 20, 2015
Michael Pacey	"Stovepipe" *The New Quarterly* Winter 2015
Trisha Rose	"Woman at the Makeup Counter in London Drugs" *Room* Vol. 38.3
Stuart Ross	"The Hanging" *The Malahat Review* Summer 2015
Robyn Sarah	"Belief" *Canadian Notes & Queries* Summer 2015
Brenda Schmidt	"Not Healing" *Puritan* Fall 2015

The Antigonish Review. PO Box 5000, Antigonish, NS B2G 2W5. antigonishreview.com

Arc Poetry Magazine. PO Box 81060, Ottawa, ON K1P 1B1. arcpoetry.ca

Ascent Aspirations. ascentaspirations.ca

Branch Magazine. branchmagazine.tumblr.com

Brick. PO Box 609, Stn. P, Toronto, ON M5S 2Y4. brickmag.com

Canadian Literature. University of British Columbia, 8-6303 N.W. Marine Dr., Vancouver, BC V6T 1Z1. canlit.ca

Canadian Notes & Queries. 1520 Wyandotte St. East, Windsor, ON, N9A 3L2. notesandqueries.ca

Canadian Poetries. canadianpoetries.com

The Capilano Review. 102-281 Industrial Ave., Vancouver, BC V6A 2P2. thecapilanoreview.ca

Carousel. UC 274, University of Guelph, Guelph, ON N1G 2W1. carouselmagazine.ca

Canadian Broadcasting Corporation CBC Poetry Prize finalists. cbc.ca

C Magazine. cmagazine.com

Contemporary Verse 2 (CV2). 502-100 Arthur St., Winnipeg, MB R3B 1H3. contemporaryverse2.ca

Descant. descant.ca (now defunct)

ditch. ditchpoetry.com (now defunct but copyright renewed in 2015)

enRoute Magazine. Spafax Canada, 4200 Boul. Saint-Laurent, Ste. 707, Montréal, QC H2W 2R2. enroute.aircanada.com

Event. PO Box 2503, New Westminster, BC V3L 5B2. event.douglas.bc.ca

Exile Quarterly. Exile/Excelsior Publishing Inc., 134 Eastbourne Ave., Toronto, ON M5P 2G6. exilequarterly.com/quarterly

Existere. Vanier College 101E, York University, 4700 Keele St. Toronto, ON M3J 1P3. yorku.ca/existere

The Fiddlehead. Campus House, University of New Brunswick, 11 Garland Ct., PO Box 4400, Fredericton, NB E3B 5A3. thefiddlehead.ca

filling Station. PO Box 22135, Bankers Hall, Calgary, AB T2P 4J5. fillingstation.ca

Forget Magazine. 810-1111, Melville St., Vancouver, B.C. V6E 3V6 forgetmagazine.com

Freefall Magazine. 922-9 Ave. SE, Calgary, AB, T2G 0S4. freefallmagazine.ca

Geist. Suite 210, 111 W. Hastings St., Vancouver, BC V6B 1H4. geist.com

Grain. PO Box 3986, Regina, SK, S4P 3R9. grainmagazine.ca

Hazlitt. penguinrandomhouse.ca/hazlitt

The Humber Literary Review. humerliteraryreview.com

The Impressment Gang. theimpressmentgang.com

The Leaf. PO Box 2259, Port Elgin, ON N0H 2C0. tiffanyweb.bmts.com/~brucedale/leaf.htm

Lemon Hound. lemonhound.com (now defunct)

The Literary Review of Canada. 706-170 Bloor St. W., Toronto, ON M5S 1T9. reviewcanada.ca

Maisonneuve. 1051 boul. Decarie, PO Box 53527, Saint Laurent, QC H4L 5J9 maisonneuve.org.

The Malahat Review. University of Victoria, PO Box 1700, Stn. CSC, Victoria, BC V8W 2Y2. malahatreview.ca

Maple Tree Literary Supplement. 1103-1701 Kilborn Ave., Ottawa, ON K1H 6M8. mtls.ca

Matrix. 1455 Blvd. de Maisonneuve, Montreal, QC H3G 1M8 matrixmagazine.org

New Poetry. newpoetry.ca

The New Quarterly. St. Jerome's University, 290 Westmount Rd. N, Waterloo, ON N2L 3G3. tnq.ca

Numéro Cinq. numerocinqmagazine.com

One Throne. onethrone.com

ottawater. ottawater.com

Our Times. 407-15 Gervais Dr., Toronto, ON M3C 1Y8. ourtimes.ca

(parenthetical). wordsonpagespress.com/parenthetical

Partisan partisanmagazine.com

Poetry Is Dead. 5020 Frances St., Burnaby, BC V5B 1T3. www.poetryisdead.ca

Prairie Fire. 423-100 Arthur St., Winnipeg, MB R3B 1H3. prairiefire.ca

PRISM International. Creative Writing Program, University of British Columbia, Buchanan Room E462, 1866 Main Mall, Vancouver, BC V6T 1Z1. prismmagazine.ca

Pulp Literature. pulpliterature.com

The Puritan. puritan-magazine.com

Queen's Quarterly. Queen's University, 144 Barrie St., Kingston, ON K7L 3N6. queensu.ca/quarterly

Rampike. uwindsor.ca/rampike (now defunct)

Ricepaper. PO Box 74174, Hillcrest RPO, Vancouver, BC V5V 5L8. ricepapermagazine.ca

Room. PO Box 46160, Stn. D, Vancouver, BC V6J 5G5. roommagazine.com

The Rotary Dial. therotarydial.ca

The Rusty Toque. therustytoque.com

17 Seconds. ottawater.com/seventeenseconds

The Steel Chisel. thesteelchisel.ca

subTerrain. PO Box 3008, MPO, Vancouver, BC V6B 3X5. subterrain.ca

Taddle Creek. PO Box 611, Stn. P, Toronto, ON M5S 2Y4. taddlecreekmag.com

This Magazine. 417-401 Richmond St. W, Toronto, ON M5V 3A8 thismagazine.ca

Vallum. 5038 Sherbrooke W., PO BOX 23077, CP Vendome, Montreal, QC H4A 1T0. vallummag.com

The Walrus. 411 Richmond St. E., Suite B15, Toronto, ON, M5A 3S5 walrusmagazine.com

Windsor Review. Department of English, University of Windsor, 401 Sunset Ave., Windsor, ON N9B 3P4. windsorreview.wordpress.com

Untethered. alwaysuntethered.com

Zouch Magazine. zouchmagazine.com

Note: The Best Canadian Poetry series makes every effort to track down Canadian journals that publish poetry. The series relies on complimentary copies from the publications involved and are most grateful for the cooperation. If you are the editor or publisher of a magazine not listed and wish to be considered for future years, please add the Best Canadian Poetry series to your comp subscription list at the address listed in the copyright page.

PERMISSION ACKNOWLEDGEMENTS ❧

"Local History" appeared in *Hazlitt* copyright © 2015 by James Arthur. Reprinted with permission of the author.

"This Job Ends in Six Months" appeared in *Arc* copyright © 2015 by Joelle Barron. Reprinted with permission of the author.

"Untitled" first appeared in French as "Sans titre" in *Poème Sale* copyright © 2014 by Hugo Beauchemin-Lachapelle. The English translation © 2015 by Alexander Rock appeared in *The Puritan*. Reprinted with permission of the translator.

"Northern Rockies" appeared in *Lemonhound* copyright © 2015 by andrea bennett. Reprinted with permission of the author.

"Vigil" appeared in *EVENT* copyright © 2015 by Sheri Benning. Reprinted with permission of the author.

"Tetherball" by Tim Bowling from *The Duende of Tetherball*, Nightwood Editions, 2016, copyright © 2016 by Tim Bowling, www.nightwoodeditions. com. Used with permission of the publisher. "Tetherball" appeared in *The Fiddlehead*.

"Flipped" appeared in *Rusty Toque* copyright © 2015 by Julie Bruck. Reprinted with permission of the author.

"Dream Jobs" from *A Pillow Book* copyright © 2016, by Suzanne Buffam. Reprinted by permission of House of Anansi Press Inc., Toronto. www. houseofanansi.com. "Dream Jobs" appeared in *The Walrus*.

"Black Sea Nettle" appeared in *PRISM* copyright © 2015 by Dani Couture. Reprinted with permission of the author.

"Modestine" appeared in *The Walrus* copyright © 2015 by Lynn Crosbie. Reprinted with permission of the author.

LIVEJOURNAL.COM/LONELYRADIO appeared in *The Puritan* © 2015 by Kayla Czaga. Reprinted with permission of the author.

Helen Humphreys is the award-winning author of four books of poetry, seven novels, and three works of creative non-fiction. Her most recent works are *The Evening Chorus* (HarperCollins, 2015) and *The River* (ECW Press, 2015). She lives in Kingston, Ontario, where she is also the city's Poet Laureate.

Anita Lahey is a poet, journalist, reviewer, and essayist. She is the author of *The Mystery Shopping Cart: Essays on Poetry and Culture* (Palimpsest Press, 2013) and of two Véhicule Press poetry collections: *Out to Dry in Cape Breton* (2006) and *Spinning Side Kick* (2011). The former was shortlisted for the Trillium Book Award for Poetry and the Ottawa Book Award.

Molly Peacock is a widely anthologized poet who writes biography, memoir, and fiction. Her newest work is *Alphabetique: 26 Characteristic Fictions*, with illustrations by Kara Kosaka. She is also the author of *The Paper Garden: Mrs. Delany Begins Her Life's Work at 72*, both from McClelland and Stewart. Her forthcoming book of poetry is *The Analyst*, poems about psychoanalysis, poetry and painting, from W.W. Norton and Biblioasis. She is the subject of Jason Guriel's monograph, *Molly Peacock: A Critical Introduction*.